MYSTERIOUS
ALBERTA

Myths, Murders, Mysteries and Legends

Lisa Wojna

QUAGMIRE PRESS

The Publisher: Quagmire Press Ltd.
Website: www.quagmirepress.com

Library and Archives Canada Cataloguing in Publication

Wojna, Lisa, 1962–, author
   Mysterious Alberta / Lisa Wojna.

Includes bibliographical references.

ISBN 978-1-926695-21-1 (pbk.)

   1. Curiosities and wonders—Alberta. 2. Alberta—Miscellanea. I. Title.

FC3661.8.W65 2013   001.94'097123   C2013-906160-6

Project Director: Hank Boer
Project Editor: Kathy van Denderen
Front and Back Cover Images: Hoodoos © BGSmith/Shutterstock; background sky © Photos.com
Photo Credits: Every effort has been made to accurately credit the sources of photographs. Any errors or omissions should be reported directly to the publisher for correction in future editions. Photographs courtesy of Glenbow Archives, Calgary (p. 89, NA-411-6; p. 92, NA-3011-16); National Research Council of Canada (pp. 223, 226, 231); Shuttershock (p. 32, 134850794); Lisa Wojna (pp. 36, 38, 82, 84, 85, 97, 101, 201, 204, 209, 240, 250).

Produced with the assistance of the Government of Alberta, Alberta Media Fund.

PC: 24

Dedication

~

For you, Mama—90 years old and still one of the most
inquisitive adventurers I've ever known.
And for you, Jada, my eight-year-old angel.
Thank you both for riding this rollercoaster with me.

Contents

Murders, Mayhem and Mysteries of the Human Kind   139

Manufactured Mysteries   198

Acknowledgements

~

There are always so many people to thank following the completion of any book, but my thank-you list for this project is considerably larger than most. The road trip I embarked upon to gain a more intimate glimpse of some of Alberta's amazing mysteries has afforded me the privilege of meeting many wonderful people. In particular, I'd like to thank Joey Ambrosi, interpretation and education officer at the Frank Slide Interpretive Centre, for all his insight and wealth of knowledge of the history behind this tragic event in Canadian history. My appreciation also goes out to Fred Dayman, former owner of the Rosedeer Hotel in Wayne, Alberta. Thanks to his direction, my cohorts and I trudged the steep hillsides surrounding this "ghost" town to visit the final resting place of many of Wayne's former residents.

Thank you, Joanna Northover, education specialist with the Royal Tyrrell Museum, for your patience with my several phone calls and emails, as well as Kelly Eddy, and Jaffra Markotic, tour guide extraordinaire with the Atlas Coal Mine National Historic Site—you really know how to spin a yarn. A sincere thanks also goes out to Ward Hughson, aquatic specialist with Jasper National Park, the informative staff at the Bar U ranch, my helpful archivist at the Alberta Provincial Police Archives, and Monica at the *Leduc Representative*.

Thank you to all the journalists and writers who have chronicled these stories in several forms throughout the years.

ACKNOWLEDGEMENTS

Although information often differs from source to source, the details gathered from these various media have enabled me to piece together several theories on some of these mysteries and, inevitably, allow you, the reader, to draw your own conclusions about the mysteries that still need solving.

Thank you goes out to Lynn Hickox, also known as "Supergranny," a modern-day explorer who has added one of the more recent mysteries to the annals of Alberta's unknowns and, in the process, has managed to carve a place for herself in the province's history.

Thank you to Garry, who loves to drive but didn't so much enjoy listening to my directions during our journey, and to Richard, who suffered alongside him.

Thank you to the staff of Quagmire Press, who believed in this project, and to Kathy van Denderen, my editor. A good book idea only becomes a great read with the keen eye and ordered mind of a talented editor. Thank you from the bottom of my heart—it's nice to dance with you again!

And, as always, thank you to my dear family. Without you, this and everything else I do would be meaningless.

Namaste.

Introduction

~

I n 2003, I served as the editor of *Central Alberta Farmer*, a local newspaper published in Leduc. It was a fantastic job that allowed me to travel through a great many of the small towns and rural communities that make up the central part of Alberta.

My husband loved my job, too. He is the ultimate Sunday driver; his all-time favourite pastime is taking the car out and just exploring. So when I had an assignment that coincided with his days off, he frequently acted as my chauffeur, which was a big relief for me because I hate driving.

One Sunday in February, we had travelled to a couple of events I needed to cover in Red Deer and Ponoka. As we began to make our way home, Garry decided to veer off the main highway to take another route, and I started dozing off, something I usually do when I sit in the passenger seat. At some point in our travels, Garry hit a gravel road, jolting me awake just in time for me to notice him doing that rubber-necking thing he does so well when he drives. He hesitantly tapped the brakes, then stepped on the gas, then tapped the brakes again. By this point, having been roused from my satisfying slumber, I was getting a little irritated.

"What's wrong?" I asked.

"I think I saw a steam engine in the front yard of the farm we just passed," he replied.

I have to admit that after a day of photographing and taking notes, I wasn't feeling up to another adventure. Garry must have felt the same as I did because he couldn't decide whether he wanted to stop the car and turn around or keep on going.

Nonetheless, I started thinking. The newspaper I worked for primarily focused on agriculture and farming stories, but I liked to include some human-interest articles in every issue. "Maybe we should turn around and take a look," I suggested. Who knows, maybe the owner of that property would give me an interview, and I could write about why someone would have a full-sized steam engine as a lawn ornament in the middle of rural Alberta?

Garry turned the car around and backtracked the kilometre or so down that gravel road to check out if he really saw what he thought he saw. That full-sized, antique steam engine gracing the front of the property wasn't the only mystery we were about to uncover—nor was it the most bizarre mystery of the day.

Peeling Back the Layers

I like to think I have an adventurous disposition, but the shyer half of my personality means it takes a bit to get me going. Although we quickly found the steam engine—it was kind of hard to miss—apprehension was mounting in my chest as we started rolling down the rural driveway.

Now, I know what you might be thinking: aren't journalists supposed to have a "do anything it takes to get a story" mentality? Yes, that's true. But it doesn't mean there aren't shy journalists out there, and I just happened to be one of them. Besides, I would argue that a good journalist also has a strong "spidey" sense, and mine was tingling out of control. What kind of person has a real, full-sized steam engine on his lawn? Someone who owned such a unique front yard accessory had to be, at the very least, quite eccentric. I mean, how much does a steam engine cost, anyway? Granted, this one wasn't operational, but its body was pristine, and it was expertly perched on an actual stretch of track. A chunk of steel that large had to cost a pretty penny, and that wasn't the only train-related item attached to this property. As we got closer to the farmhouse, we noticed that the train theme extended beyond the steam engine, as there was a miniature train track circling the yard, complete with a miniature train to go with it.

What other treasures might we find tucked away on this acreage?

No one answered the door when we knocked. A mixture of disappointment and relief flooded over me when, as we turned to leave, a battered pickup truck rolled in and parked right behind our car. A young girl barely tall enough to see over the steering wheel tumbled out of the driver's seat. And when a much older man stepped out from the passenger's side of the truck, my initial bent toward caution in this scenario accelerated into the red zone. The man might have been a senior, but he looked tough, and I was sure he was giving us that "Who do you think you are venturing onto my property uninvited?" and "Don't mess with me" kind of stare.

As it turned out, once I introduced myself and stated my reason for being on his property, the gent was friendly enough.

He was only too happy to answer all of my questions about the steam engine and the child-sized train circling his yard. He talked about his love for locomotives and how his grandkids had so enjoyed tooling around on the small train when they were younger. It was clear the man could have spoken endlessly on the subject. I started to thank him for his time, and he asked us if we'd like to see some of his other collectables.

Garry and I looked at each other, wondering what other eccentricities might be discovered on the senior's property. "Sure," I said as we started walking west of the house to the nearest of several farm buildings that all looked the same and reminded me of the several, innocuous sheds that once dotted my grandfather's property.

Nothing could have prepared us for what we saw.

"This is my special collection," he said as he hauled open the weathered door of the farm building. When I finally recovered from the shock of seeing a full-sized Nazi flag pinned across the back wall, the contents of the display cases in the room flustered me further. There were assorted hand grenades, a uniform that, according to our host, once belonged to a Nazi general, German handguns, a copy of *Mein Kampf* and countless other German-related World War II paraphernalia. This wasn't at all what I had bargained for in a human-interest story of rural origins.

And it only got more interesting from there.

We moved on to other barns, each one containing a treasure trove of collectibles of their own. One building housed a variety of antiques but also included a one-of-a-kind coffin the gent was building for his "big day." Another barn boasted an assortment of archaeological artifacts that, according to the owner, several academics from various universities had examined. He said these specialists hinted that the strange-looking rock formations, which had been dug from his fields not far from where we stood, might have been of alien origin. Another, much larger outbuilding housed a vast selection of antique farm equipment, and I couldn't help but think that the curators at the Reynolds-Alberta Museum would have loved a chance to acquire one of those items for their collection, including a piece that the man claimed was an engine from the original Avro Arrow. The Avro Arrow was a hypersonic fighter jet that, when it was built in 1958, represented the cutting edge in aircraft technology. Designed and built in Canada, by Canadian aircraft manufacturer A.V. Roe Canada, the jet represented a "crowning jewel" in this country's aerospace technology. And yet, shortly after its successful test flight, the project was mysteriously cancelled and all known engines and plans destroyed. How was it, then, that this man had what he claimed to be an original engine from the plane?

And just when we thought we'd seen it all, the man asked us if we'd like to tour his bomb shelter, located beneath his home. By this point, my shyness had evaporated. I was no longer tired, and I didn't hesitate to take him up on his offer.

A baby grand piano graced the entire living room floor of the old farmhouse. The man even played a song for us before he asked us to squeeze around the piano and into a room that looked somewhat like a library from an Agatha Christie made-for-TV movie. It was a little disconcerting to be sandwiched in such a small space with this man. We'd assumed we'd be going down-stairs to a bomb shelter, but a quick glance around the room didn't suggest any access to the basement. The gent then grabbed one of the bookshelves and pulled, revealing a secret passageway.

"Cool!" I said, leaving Garry at the top of the narrow stairway as I descended into the darkness, my guide behind me. He explained that despite the cold, damp environment, the underground shelter, with its cement walls, would be self-sustaining should an atomic bomb be dropped in Canada. There was an assortment of batteries and mechanical objects along with shelves lined with canned goods that look liked they could, quite conceivably, have been around since the 1960s when the Cold War era was in full swing and the shelter was built.

"This shelter is one of a very few shelters of its kind," the man said, explaining how he had some kind of contract with the government of the time to construct this safe haven.

Meanwhile, somewhere at the entrance to the shelter, Garry was waiting—and probably worrying about my safety. I must have sensed his unease because as I was walking the long and narrow underground room, I felt a sudden urge to leave.

Garry and I wanted to get out of there, but our guide stood between us and the front door. At some point between the time we watched the man's half-ton pull into the driveway and the hour or so we were at the farmhouse, the young girl driving the truck, who our guide introduced as his granddaughter, had disappeared.

It was dark by now, and we were alone. The truck was still parked behind our car.

And the man who gave us a tour of his home now had a gun in his hand.

"This," he said, holding a lady's white-handled gun in his palm, finger on the trigger, "once belonged to Hitler's secretary. She lived not far from here, you know. Of course, that was never public knowledge."

Garry and I looked at each other—we didn't need to speak.

Segments of this experience propelled me into a kind of intrigue I'd only read about in books, and I was grateful for the opportunity. But the entire evening was so shrouded in mystery it was as if Garry and I were living in a dream, and at times I worried that I'd never see my kids again.

Our experience that day was something we shared with anyone who would listen, time and time again. I also included the story in the pages of *Central Alberta Farmer*, minus any reference to the World War II paraphernalia and the Avro Arrow engine. In fact, I emailed the producers of the TV series *Canadian Pickers*, suggesting their crew might be interested in touring the place themselves; although I'm not an expert in antiques, I have no doubt that a great many rare objects were housed on the acreage.

Garry and I stumbled onto that property more than 10 years ago, but we still reminisce about it from time to time. In many ways, it feels as though it just happened yesterday.

Garry has tried several times to find that side road again, and the property with a train engine that couldn't be moved all that easily, but without success.

We have no doubt that we visited this property—we have pictures to prove it. But the answers to the questions that arose during our visit, and afterward, remained a mystery to us.

Who was this man who led us through his rural acreage and shared so much of himself, and what other secrets might he have locked away? Did a woman who once served as Hitler's secretary really live a few kilometres from his property? And had she really owned the small pistol the farmer showed us?

Did aliens really land on his property decades earlier, only to leave behind a selection of unique stone carvings? Where did this gent get all his Nazi paraphernalia, especially a fully decorated general's uniform? And was he really contracted by the government to build his underground bunker back in the 1960s, or was he just a survivalist with an agenda of his own?

When I began writing *Mysterious Alberta*, the story of this unique encounter served as a catalyst of sorts for me. I thought if I could stumble across something so out of the ordinary during a simple Sunday drive, there was no telling what other amazing stories I might be able to dig up.

I wasn't disappointed.

Whether it's the land, the people, the creations we've made, the secret government activities or unexplained phenomena attributed to otherworldly encounters, mysteries abound in this province. And for the purpose of this book, these mysteries include anything secret, unexplained, unknown, obscure or puzzling, or any problem or conundrum that occurs naturally or is a result of our interactions with nature and with each other.

FROM ANOTHER
DIMENSION

Chapter One

Going Wendigo

~

The Weendigo [sic] *was gaunt to the point of emaciation, its desiccated skin pulled tautly over its bones. With its bones pushing out against its skin, its complexion the ash gray of death, and its eyes pushed back deep into their sockets, the Weendigo looked like a gaunt skeleton recently disinterred from the grave. What lips it had were tattered and bloody.... Unclean and suffering from suppurations of the flesh, the Weendigo gave off a strange and eerie odor of decay and decomposition, of death and corruption...*

–excerpt from *Manitous: The Spiritual World of the Ojibway* by Basil Johnston

~

The winter of 1878 was a particularly cold one for residents of northcentral Alberta. Although weather conditions are less extreme in this part of the province than farther north, the mercury often dips as low as –30°C. Add in the wind chill factor, and it feels 10 degrees cooler.

The bitter cold that winter made it impossible for even the bravest hunter to venture out to find dinner. Ka-Ki-Si-Sutchin would have preferred to huddle among his people, or lodge in one of the new settlements in the area rather than hunt for food and crowd into a makeshift hut.

Things didn't have to be so difficult, Ka-Ki-Si-Sutchin knew. Known as Swift Runner by members of the North-West Mounted Police (NWMP), Ka-Ki-Si-Sutchin had made a good life for himself and his ever-burgeoning family. The 6-foot, 3-inch Cree had served as a guide for the officers since the force arrived in that part of Alberta five years earlier, and he was generally well liked throughout the settlement he called home, located near present-day Fort Saskatchewan. He was a skilled trapper, the type of man the NWMP needed to call on from time to time, and he was paid well for his hunting skills. He was proud of his ability to provide for his wife and six children, as well as his mother and brother.

But Swift Runner developed a love for the taste of whisky, and it transformed him into a feral monster. He became so uncontrollable that despite his family's connections, the members of his tribe didn't want him around when he was under the influence. It was his own fault that he and his family were banished to the backcountry.

Any other year and it wouldn't have been such an insufferable sentence, but that winter was different, and Swift Runner had a hard time identifying the cause of his melancholy. Usually the wilderness was a peaceful place for the man who made his money scouting and trapping, but a growing anxiety was making him more and more edgy each day. The woods called to him, but the whispers weren't the gentle ones he was used to. Instead, he felt a growing sense of ill ease with each rustle of leaves, each snap of a twig, each mournful groaning of the trees as they were jostled about by the wind.

Then there was the creature. Nobody else had noticed it, but Swift Runner had seen it lurking about, and it was calling to him—it was invading his dreams. It was relentless. But Swift Runner figured out a way to silence it. The only problem was that once Swift Runner followed through with what he felt the creature was pressing him to do, he was alone. He no longer heard the chatter of his children at play. His mother and brother were gone. His wife was no more.

Even the voices had left him.

The Story Behind the Silence

When Swift Runner arrived at the Catholic Mission in St. Albert as the snow was melting in early 1879, he received a warm, albeit tentative, welcome. People thought it odd that he was alone. Where were his wife and six children, his brother and mother?

"Dead," Swift Runner explained in a muffled voice. "All dead."

When the priests at the mission asked him what had happened, Swift Runner said his wife had committed suicide, and the rest of his family had died of starvation. The man's story didn't make sense. Swift Runner's family had been in good health when they were last seen the previous winter, and the 200-pound man didn't look as if he'd gone without food. The story didn't ring true. The priests shared their suspicions with the North-West Mounted Police who, in turn, questioned Swift Runner on the matter. The officers must have agreed that Swift Runner's story needed to be verified, and a trip to the man's campsite was organized.

When the search party arrived at Swift Runner's winter camp, they noticed a mound of earth that looked like a grave. It *was* a grave, Swift Runner explained. One of his sons had died in the winter, and that was where he'd been interred. When the officers dug up the grave, they found the intact body of a young boy, and there didn't appear to be anything suspicious about his death.

The bleached bones littering the campsite, on the other hand, were an altogether different matter.

Inspector Severe Gagnon was one of the officers accompanying Swift Runner that day. When he asked the trapper about the moccasin-stuffed human skull he'd just picked up, Gagnon was startled by the man's honest reply.

It was his dead wife's skull. The smaller bones belonged to his children, the others to his brother and mother. Aside from the bones, so bare even the marrow was gone, there were no other signs of Swift Runner's family.

Nothing could have prepared Gagnon for Swift Runner's story.

It was the spirit of Wendigo, the man explained. Wendigo had taken over Swift Runner's body and, hungry for human flesh, forced the man to kill and consume each member of his family, with the exception of the son who had died before the carnage began.

Swift Runner's brother was the first to die. Author Bruce Wishart explained that Swift Runner told the officers present that Wendigo had forced one of Swift Runner's boys to "kill and butcher his younger brother" and then the spirit had forced Swift Runner to hang the man's "infant by the neck from a lodge pole and [tug] at the baby's dangling feet."

Bowled over by Swift Runner's candid confession, the officers collected whatever bones hadn't been dragged away by wild animals and returned with the man to Fort Saskatchewan. It's impossible to imagine the waves of emotion that overtook those who viewed the site and heard the tale surrounding the deaths of so many innocent people (sources vary between seven and eight murders attributed to the man). It's equally impossible to assess how the seemingly distraught husband and father must have felt. However, there was no question—Swift Runner had to be taken into custody, and a jury would have to decide his fate.

Vicious Demon

Author and Native scholar Basil Johnston, in his book, *The Manitous: The Spiritual World of the Ojibway*, explains that of all "the evil beings who dwelt on the periphery of the world of the Anishinaubae peoples, none was more terrifying than the Weendigo. It was a creature loathsome to behold and as loathsome in its habits, conduct and manners."

Many First Nations legends throughout the northern U.S. and parts of Canada describe the spirit of Wendigo (which is spelled several different ways) as a cannibalistic demon that is never satisfied with anything but human flesh. He is large, "five to eight times above the height of a tall man," and grows larger with every killing, and in so doing, is constantly hungry for more. He is the personification of greed and excess. Cultures sharing the Wendigo legend also held the belief that the spirit could possess people, who in turn, would embody its characteristics.

When someone has "gone Wendigo," they become obsessed with the hunger for human flesh. As with the spirit in the legend, other food will not quench this desire, which has been termed by some as "Wendigo psychosis." One source suggests that the psychosis is a "culture-bound syndrome," but whether it is a legitimate disorder continues to be a matter of much debate.

The fear of being attacked by the spirit was very much a part of the culture in northern Alberta's Aboriginal communities in the late 19th century. A person was at risk of possession by the demon when he or she started feeling the draw toward cannibalism. In some cases, victims of the spirit would complain about physical changes. When these symptoms occurred, the victims often turned to the Native healer of their village for help. If the urge to consume human flesh didn't subside despite help, it wasn't uncommon for the troubled individual to ask the elders of the village to take his life before he took someone else's. Other victims of this possession would kill themselves before they'd ever admit they felt compelled toward cannibalism.

Holed up in the bush for the winter, Swift Runner didn't have a healer within arm's reach when he started hearing the voices and had his strange dreams. Swift Runner was convinced Wendigo had taken over his body and mind and had committed the crimes.

Swift Runner repeatedly expressed regret over his actions, to the police and later to the guards monitoring his jail cell. "The least of men," he reportedly called himself and said, "[I] do not merit even being called a man." Swift Runner didn't mount a defence at his trial; he simply admitted to the crimes when asked if he had anything to say. Swift Runner never wavered from his story. He was distraught over the deaths of his family members and ashamed that he couldn't fight off the monster in his mind. He had been too weak.

Swift Runner's confession and subsequent remorse were of no real concern when he went to trial on August 8, 1879. The father-turned-cannibal faced a jury of his peers, both Cree and Métis. They knew of the Wendigo legends, but you can't punish a spirit; Swift Runner was found guilty of the murder of five of his children as well as his wife, brother and mother.

He was sentenced to die; his death would be the first "legal hanging" in what is now Alberta. A special gallows was erected in Fort Saskatchewan, and the last chapter to Swift Runner's saga occurred on December 20, 1879.

The Alberta trapper wasn't the first to succumb to the nefarious spirit, but most of the victims who died were executed before they committed the kinds of evil for which Swift Runner will forever be remembered. The elders of several First Nations communities still speak of Wendigo, and the Anishinaubae people still perform ceremonial dances to remind them of Wendigo's strength and the dangers of excess.

Is there a cannibalistic demon called Wendigo? And was Swift Runner nothing more than a helpless puppet in a loathsome act of insatiable greed committed by a spirit far too strong for anyone to control? Moreover, is it possible that the Wendigo of legend can reach out to vulnerable people today and wield his power?

Repeat Intruder?

In the last several decades, the name "Wendigo" hasn't cast the same fear it did in days past. But the legend was resurrected in a gruesome way in July 2008.

News reports of the horrific incident that occurred that summer were so unbelievable that many who heard them might have thought reporters couldn't have possibly gotten the story right, or they had exaggerated at the very least. Surely such acts only took place in B-rated horror flicks.

Those skeptics couldn't have been more wrong.

Twenty-two-year-old Tim McLean was sleeping away his bus ride from Edmonton to his home in Winnipeg on July 30 after completing a stint as a carnival worker in Alberta. Some time after the Greyhound passed through Erickson, Manitoba, Tim roused enough to notice a middle-aged man had taken the seat next to him. Acknowledging his new seatmate, McLean stretched, shifted his position a little and then nodded off once again.

Life hadn't been easy for Vince Weiguang Li, but he was a hard worker and people liked him. He had been working in Edmonton delivering newspapers before boarding the Greyhound to Winnipeg. For some inexplicable reason, Li felt drawn to McLean. It didn't make sense, but Li was sure of what was being asked of him. Li understood that what others would call the spirit of Wendigo was God telling him McLean was a bad man. No. He wasn't a man; he was an alien. It was up to Li to save the world from the possible destruction the sleeping passenger might bring about.

Everything happened so quickly. Screams escaped the throats of neighbouring passengers before their minds could fully grasp the chaos taking place in the narrow, confined space of the Greyhound bus.

There were other sounds, too—the gargled gasps of an innocent victim, shocked awake by a knife cutting through his throat. What was happening? God willing, McLean never fully understood his fate before Li's knife made the final cut and beheaded him.

News reports at the time ran "graphic content" warnings alongside the headlines of stories covering the grizzly murder that shocked the nation—and the world. The victim and perpetrator didn't know each other, and no amount of reasoning could explain why Li butchered McLean and put parts of his body in plastic bags that he then scattered throughout the murder scene. McLean's eyes and heart were never recovered. Although people speculated about what happened to these body parts, the details were never disclosed to the public. It has been suggested that Li consumed some of them.

The judicial aftermath of the horrible crime that claimed the life of an innocent man found Li not criminally responsible for his actions; he was diagnosed with schizophrenia and incarcerated in Manitoba's Selkirk Mental Health Centre. But the events leading up to the murder were, for some, more than merely coincidental. For people like Nathan Carlson, who was all too aware of the legend of Wendigo, those events were proof positive that the evil creature had returned to claim another victim.

"Ever since it happened, I haven't been able to get it out of my head," Carlson told *Sun* reporter Andrew Hanon.

No one would fault Carlson for his tribulations. Ten days before Tim McLean's murder, the historian, touted as one of the "world's leading authorities on Wendigo," spoke with Hanon about the monster's lust for human flesh. Hanon was writing an article about Swift Runner and the murders of his family members, and Hanon sought out Carlson for his take on the subject. The two had talked about Swift Runner; they spoke of how Wendigo, over time, had been blamed for many unexplained and gruesome murders in the northern U.S. and Canada.

When that story went to press on July 20, no one could have known that an unassuming man named Vince Li would be delivering copies of that issue of the *Sun* throughout Edmonton. And that 10 days later, Li would commit an atrocity of unmitigated proportions of his own. And just like Swift Runner, Li would beg for someone to end his life.

Hanon examined the parallel between the two stories, but nothing suggests Li had read the July 20 account of Wendigo. Still, some who witness or write about these crimes feel a need to draw the parallels and, like the Anishinaubae who continue to perform their ceremonial dances, warn others.

As Carlson said, mulling on the juxtaposition between his interview with Hanon and the horrific event that hot July night, "There are just too many coincidences…it's beyond eerie."

Chapter Two

Ghostly Encounters

~

I had three short dreams on three separate nights.

In the first dream, a frisky orange kitten scurries across a room in pursuit of a baby-blue locust. The kitten catches and eats the unlucky insect and immediately transforms into a fully grown black cat, and a bitter smell bites at my nostrils.

In the second dream, I am ascending the winding staircase of the turret of a stone castle when I am suddenly suctioned by an unknown force and pulled backwards down the same staircase. As I descend, I pass by my mother and sister. We make eye contact, but they are unable to reach out to help me, and I continue falling as if into a dark abyss.

In the final dream, I am at church. I've brought a friend— a beautiful young girl with strawberry-blonde hair. We go up to the altar railing, and after consuming the host she receives from the green-eyed, dark-bearded priest, her hair changes colour. Her long locks turn raven-black, and flow, thick and shiny, down the back of the purple satin gown she wears. Paralyzed with fear, I can't breathe, and when I am jolted awake, I see the shadow of what looks like a troll sitting by my side. Turning into my pillow, I pray. The image vanishes as quickly as it appeared, but I am left shaken.

~

Everyone dreams, and most of us would agree that the dreams we remember rarely make sense. But something was different about the three dreams I experienced, described above. They were interconnected somehow. And when I shared my dreams with a woman I felt was knowledgeable in the spiritual realm, she agreed.

Unlike the dreams possessing Swift Runner, as mentioned in the previous chapter, the dreams I'd experienced were warning dreams. "God is trying to protect you from something," my friend said.

Weeks went by, and because the dreams had stopped, I forgot about them until I experienced a personal crisis that spelled the end of my first marriage. I remembered the dreams then. Now they made so much more sense to me. And I realized my friend was right—I had been warned.

Belief in a spiritual dimension is an incredibly vast and personal subject. Some of us believe that energy never dies, and that because we are made of energy, our souls will live on in another realm after we die and may reappear from time to time in the form of ethereal apparitions. Others adhere to the beliefs of their own faith and rarely veer from the doctrines of their particular religion. Still others believe there's room for diversity, or the melding of kindred faith interpretations, and may embrace a wide variety of beliefs concurrently. And then there are the diehard skeptics who might happily chime in with Ebenezer Scrooge when he discounts the spirit of his business partner Jacob Marley, calling it "an undigested bit of beef, a blot of mustard, a crumb of cheese, a fragment of underdone potato. There's more of gravy than of grave about you, whatever you are!"

Accounts of apparitions and other unexplained disturbances are unsettling because many of these alleged hauntings are thought to represent angry spirits. The theory is that during their earthly existence, these spirits may have experienced some kind of unresolved evil and are looking for a way to find peace.

Happy spirits, on the other hand, are contented spirits, so they have no need to be heard, or perhaps their role is more of a protective one, and they are watching over us, like angels.

As you read through the accounts that follow, you'll see why they are wrapped in controversy. Whatever your belief about ghosts, the people mentioned in the stories believe their experiences were genuine. The unexplained reports that are told around campfires and handed down from generation to generation represent just a small sample of Alberta's ghost stories.

Banff Springs Hotel

When Chip Coffey, the self-proclaimed psychic and host of the A&E shows *Paranormal State* and *Psychic Kids,* arrived at the Banff Springs Hotel in June 2010, he immediately added to the backstory of one of its more infamous ghostly residents. Legend has it that in 1932, a bride died on her wedding night when she fell down the stairs after her wedding gown, which had brushed against the open flame of a candle, caught fire. Her name was Christina, and Coffey bonded so firmly with her spirit just minutes after his arrival that she told him something only her mother and fiancé had known—she had been pregnant when she died.

Coffey was visiting the mountain town during the Banff World Television Festival when he spoke with *Calgary Herald* reporter Eric Volmers. Reflecting on the colourful history of the hotel, which opened in 1888, Coffey said that Christina was the first of many apparitions he met during the annual conference.

The ghosts that reside at the Banff Springs Hotel aren't a shy lot. Based on the number of people who've reported seeing the vision of a young woman in a flowing white gown, Christina seems to mingle with the guests on a regular basis. The first sighting of Christina took place a year after her death. Since then, many of the hotel's visitors have seen her floating down the hotel's main staircase and dancing in the ballroom.

But other wandering spirits enjoy meeting the public every now and again, and the next legendary apparition can be traced back to a Banff-area resident.

Sam McAuley was a bellman at the Banff Springs Hotel for the majority of his working life. By all accounts he loved his job so much that every time he retired, which apparently happened more than once, he was so distressed by the perceived void in his life that he returned to work in short order.

One account states that during his lengthy employment at the historic establishment, McAuley often joked he'd never leave the place and would continue with his duties long after he died. Perhaps it wasn't surprising, then, that shortly after his death in 1975, the first stories about a ghostly bellman wandering the halls began to circulate—he was referred to as a "ghost" because some witnesses described him as a "transparent" figure.

But the vision of an elderly man dressed in an old-fashioned bellman uniform wasn't always a ghostly image witnessed from a distance; at times it was impossible to distinguish between the apparition and a real person.

Such was the case when two women called down to the Banff Springs front desk asking for help not long after Sam's death. The women had locked their keys in the hotel room and

Legend has it that the mysterious Banff Springs Hotel lures an assortment of visitors of the long-deceased kind.

needed someone to open the door. When one of the hotel's staff arrived at their suite, he was surprised to find the women inside the room. A kind and helpful elderly bellman had already come to the women's aid and opened the door for them, they explained. The problem was, the hotel hadn't had an elderly bellman on staff since McAuley's death. When asked to describe the man in question, the women provided a description that sounded a lot like McAuley. It appeared the man was being true to his word and was reaching out from beyond the grave.

Sam sightings continue to trickle in from time to time, and in each report, McAuley is happily carrying out the duties he'd diligently performed his entire earthly career. He has been seen greeting guests and carrying luggage from the front foyer to the guests' suites, but he always disappears before the guests can give him a tip. One report even tells of how a bellman matching Sam's description was seen walking through a wall—evidently he was eager to attend to an important matter and decided to take advantage of his ghostly status by taking a shortcut.

But not all of the supernatural beings at the famous, majestic hotel were as gentle and helpful as Sam or as harmless as Christine dancing in the ballroom. A far more gruesome event is rumoured to have taken place in room 873.

If you visit the hotel, you'll notice that room number 873 does not exist. At one time, after an entire family was murdered in the suite, the room was boarded up. One reason for this drastic measure centred around the claim that a child's fingerprints would randomly appear on the walls and mirror of the hotel room. It was a constant reminder of the tragedy for staff, who couldn't seem to get rid of the prints entirely, and was disturbing to guests who learned of the story. No one wanted to stay in the room—sometimes merely being in its vicinity was eerie enough. After the room was boarded up, visitors and staff alike reported seeing different family members appear in the area where the room was located. They are seen walking through the wall to the place where they died.

The stories of Sam the bellman, although anecdotal in nature, can be traced back to a former employee of the hotel. The gruesome mass murder of an entire family should be traceable as well—it should have been recorded in the annals of a small-town newspaper somewhere. Unfortunately, any concrete proof to substantiate this story, including the time when the murders might have taken place, has eluded investigators. Did hotel management really board up a room where such a heinous event occurred? Or is the "missing room" the result of an error made by the building contractors? Did the murder of a family, or any murder whatsoever, actually take place anywhere in the hotel? Or are there some other reasons for the unexplained sightings attributed to room 873?

Banff's well-storied spirits are so popular among paranormal groups that doctors Dave Oester and Sharon Gill of the International Ghost Hunters Society descended on the famous hotel to check out the metaphysical activity for themselves. Using an assortment of electronic equipment, the two researchers scouted the premises for "sudden changes in temperatures or electromagnetic fields." According to TaxiMike.com, a website dedicated to all things Banff, significant readings in these fields could "indicate the presence of ghostly entities." Photographs taken during these visits showed unexplained effects, including "an ectoplasmic cloud" and a "strange ray of light."

Even the most cynical visitors staying at the Banff Springs Hotel have experienced hair-raising situations they couldn't brush off so easily. One example involves a businessman who, while taking his breakfast in his room one morning, felt pressure near his neck and shoulders, as if someone was pressing their hands against him. Panicked, he allegedly rushed out of his room and requested another suite.

Regardless your take on ghosts and the spirit world, a stay at the Banff Springs Hotel will never be disappointing— and who knows, you may get more than you've paid for.

Tarred and Feathered

A corner of Alberta that many sources claim contains "the richest dinosaur fossil beds in the world" has had its fair share of resident ghosts. One of its better-known apparitions also resides in a hotel.

When the coal mines of southern Alberta's badlands were at their height of production, the community of Wayne boasted a population of 3000. Coal was plentiful in the hillsides surrounding Wayne and its neighbouring communities, and because coal was in high demand for home heating and cooking purposes, a job in the mines was one of the more stable occupations. People arrived when the Red Deer Coal Company set up operations in 1912. Schools, stores, a hospital and a theatre were built soon after, providing the town's inhabitants with every-thing they needed for a comfortable life.

But when natural gas offered homeowners a cleaner alternative, coal production dwindled drastically, and people migrated to other communities to look for employment. The buildings in Wayne fell into disrepair, and many were eventu-ally bulldozed. Of the few original buildings that remain stand-ing, in what is now a virtual ghost town, is the Rosedeer Hotel.

The hotel boasts a decidedly more western flair than the Banff Springs Hotel. A boar's head peers out from the assort-ment of cowboy curiosities and mining gear that lines the walls of the establishment's café, and if you look close enough, you'll even come across one or two bullet holes in the walls of the Last Chance Saloon.

Opened in 1913, the Rosedeer Hotel in Wayne has seen a lot of action in its 100-year history, and some of that action hasn't always been positive. The spirit of at least one mine worker is said to roam the hallways to this day.

Although rooms on the second floor are rented out to the occasional visitor, and inquisitive ghost hunter, the third floor is closed down. Some have argued the reason for the closure is because a ghost inhabits the third floor—and he's not a gentle spirit.

According to the town's history, people migrated to Wayne because they were able to secure a steady income at the mine. And although workers were glad for their jobs, life in the coal mines wasn't easy, and the environment was often challenging. It's not surprising, then, that some employees decided to take action when management turned a deaf ear to their requests for more money and improved working conditions.

Management didn't approve of their employees' efforts to organize a union. If they heard any rumour of a mineworker rallying his colleagues, the powers that be had a sure-fire way of dealing with the troublemaker—hire a thug. The enforcer, which in this case was widely speculated to be a member of the Ku Klux Klan, would hang out in the saloon, and when he heard any talk about unions, he'd haul the man up to his room on the third floor and give the culprit a good going over. In the 1920s, one of these situations got out of control, and a man who'd been "tarred and feathered" died. It goes without saying that the spirit of the dead man would have been angry at his demise; it's his ghost that many in Wayne believe has haunted the hotel ever since.

Hotel proprietor Fred Dayman has lived in Wayne his entire life; his family has owned the hotel since it was built in 1913. Although hotel guests have often told him they've seen

Some have suggested that spirits roam the overgrown patch of land that once served as the graveyard to the small town of Wayne.

an image of the murdered man in his establishment, Dayman has never seen one himself. He doesn't doubt its existence, though. In fact, he believes spirits lurk throughout Wayne.

"The whole area is heavy with spirit," he is quoted by *Ghost Stories of Alberta* author Barbara Smith. "There was an Indian camp and graveyard nearby. There have been problems [with ghosts] there too."

Gentler Spirit

The Auditorium Hotel in Nanton, also in southern Alberta, is another public house that has seen its fair share of changes over the years. Built in 1902, the original 10-room inn was one of the few rooming houses where travellers could lay their weary heads after a long day on the road. During the course of the hotel's 111-year history, the two-storey building was expanded to include a third floor to accommodate its growing business; that third floor was later lost in a fire.

Today, the building has been restored to its original state, minus a third floor, and continues to offer visitors a place to stay. But people don't visit the Auditorium Hotel just for the beds. The local hotspot is also considered "Nanton's Entertainment Headquarters." Musicians add ambience for patrons enjoying the hotel's culinary offerings, which are reputed to be mouthwatering. And music isn't the only form of entertainment available. The Auditorium Hotel is yet another Alberta inn with a resident ghost to boast about, and in this case, the spirit's name and earthly persona is common knowledge in Nanton.

Rex Irwin was a ranch hand who worked in the area and visited the hotel on paydays. He'd put up his feet, enjoy the good food and finish his workday off with a few drinks. He wasn't the rowdy kind of drunk sometimes found in bars. But during one of his visits, Rex died in his hotel room. The legends don't give any reason for the man's death; perhaps he had a heart attack or just slipped away in his sleep. It has been widely reported that although his body was interred, his spirit never left this earth.

It's quite likely that had Rex died because of a violent altercation of some kind, his spirit would have a more threatening presence. Instead, the ghost of Rex Irwin seems to be harmless. In fact, it appears he's just hanging out at his favourite earthly establishment. Visitors at the Auditorium Hotel reported sensing his presence and, as Barbara Smith wrote in *Haunted Alberta*, if you "leave a glass of whiskey on the basement stairs, it'll be gone in the morning." Apparently Rex continues to enjoy his libations after all these years. Still, aside from sneaking a drink or two and rearranging the furniture on occasion, he's one of the more friendly ghosts a person is apt to encounter. And there have been no reports that his presence has frightened off any of the hotel's patrons.

Spirits Move into the Community

It's not just hotels in Alberta that host spirits from the afterlife. Schools, community clubs, acreages and farmhouses, individual homes and even churches have reported strange happenings within the confines of their walls. So it's not surprising to learn that hospitals—or buildings that once were hospitals—would have their fair share of ghostly happenings as well.

According to a variety of sources, the Community Cultural Centre in Brooks is no stranger to paranormal activity. The centre was originally built as a hospital, and a little boy, an elderly janitor and an old matron, along with as many as 75 spirits, have been seen at one point or another during the building's 70-year history. The community centre's visitors have described seeing a little boy with a backpack romping in the hallways as if on his way to school. A matronly woman allegedly reads a book to children she picks at random. And the janitor, a common sighting among visitors, is constantly seen mopping and cleaning, apparently sentenced to an afterlife with no retirement in sight.

Calgary's Grace Hospital is also rumoured to house at least one ghost; some sources even suggest that a monument in neighbouring Riley Park was erected in memory of a woman and child who reputedly died in the hospital during childbirth. And ever since this event, women who give birth in the same room where this sad story allegedly occurred are said to have difficult labours that frequently result in caesarean sections.

The problem with this account is that the monument was, in actual fact, commemorating the life of Maudine Riley, teacher and mother of three. And Riley did not die while giving birth; she died in 1962. Riley was a women's activist in Calgary who, along with the Famous Five, helped earn women the right to vote in 1916. However, according to a biography of Riley written by John Savoie, she and one of her babies almost died during childbirth—Paranormal Studies and Investigations Canada (PSICAN) suggest that perhaps this could be the reason for the connection.

Regardless the background of the story, a report published on PSICAN's website garnered several comments from paranormal enthusiasts who shared experiences they had at Grace Hospital. One woman, who had been admitted to the hospital for back surgery in 2000, reported seeing "a lady with dark brown hair and a white outfit on sitting in one of the chairs" in her room. The patient had returned to her room after taking a stroll in the hallway. Thinking maybe she'd misread the room number, she double-checked the number on the door.

When she confirmed the room was indeed hers, she went back inside only to find that the lady was gone.

During a casual conversation the next morning, a nurse told patients that the ghost of a woman routinely wandered "the halls looking for her baby because she died giving birth to it." In another report, a former security guard at the hospital reported unexplained sights and sounds on the maternity ward during one of his night shifts in 1995. Even though the ward was closed for the night, the television in the mothers' TV room would spontaneously turn on, and alarms would sound from various operating rooms. After a harrowing night, the guard uttered a prayer of sorts, offering compassion to the unsettled spirit and asking it to understand the chaos it was causing.

More recently, a May 20, 2012, article in the *Calgary Sun* told of several reports of unexplained experiences from Calgary's Peter Lougheed Hospital.

"We would get individuals…saying they saw ghosts and heard weird noises, they had a 'creeped-out' feeling," Dr. Lloyd Maybaum told reporter Nadia Moharib. The psychiatrist was referring to a room where a patient had committed suicide. Maybaum went on to say that several patients had shared a variety of experiences over a period of many months. From a psychological point of view, Maybaum said it's understandable that staff and patients would feel uncomfortable entering a room with that type of history. Despite the fact that hospital staff don't publicize suicides, stories of calamity trickle out from random sources, and over time develop into an urban legend of sorts. The only remedy that seemed to have a lasting effect in settling the disturbing vibes people were sensing was a pastor who was called in and asked to bless the room.

Managing spiritual care was part of the overall treatment for the sick in generations past, but with the advent of modern medicine, the spiritual aspect was forgotten for a time. Now, a renewed interest in a more holistic approach to health includes attention to the spiritual well-being of an individual. Although the spiritual interests of a patient typically focus on prayer and other religious practices, such as discussions with a hospital chaplain, an exorcism, for example, might be another form of healing as well; the patient achieves a sense of peace that traditional medicine can't always provide.

Spirit Possessions

Some authorities on the subject of ghosts and the paranormal would adamantly argue that an individual claiming to experience that type of mysterious phenomenon was possessed by the devil. Arizona-based pastor Bob Larson has visited Alberta on a number of occasions, offering his take on the subject as well as helping people who struggle with some kind of inner demon.

"What Mr. Larson does is he ministers to people with spiritual bondage in their lives…uncontrollable anger, depression, suicidal thoughts," Pastor Ron Hermann explained in a 1999 *Edmonton Sun* article. "It's a serious calling. It's what Jesus himself did."

Not every Christian would approve of Larson's methods, which includes exorcisms often assisted by three teenaged "soldiers" who are frequently referred to as "Larson's daughters." But despite the criticisms, Larson and his entourage very much believe in their ministry. "Evil is a reality—everyone faces it," Brynne Larson (Bob's daughter) told Quebecor Media Inc. reporter Thane Burnett in October 2012. "We have a choice to face it and fight or turn our back."

Throughout history, unexplained events have turned some of the most uncompromising cynics into believers. One such case involved a friend of mine who worked as a nurse in a children's ward of a hospital in the late 1980s.

This friend told me of a child she'd been caring for, and how the youngster's ailment was puzzling to the medical team involved in his care. According to my friend, the boy sporadically exhibited almost convulsive symptoms, losing control of his bodily functions and flailing about in such a frenzied manner that several people had to hold him down so he wouldn't hurt himself. My friend would enter the child's hospital room to perform a bed check, to bring in a meal or just to offer comfort, and on some of these occasions, when she called the child by name, she would get no response. Then suddenly the boy would speak in an unknown language, and although he would be staring back at her, his lips wouldn't be moving, and the voice she heard wouldn't be the child's.

At this point it would be prudent of me to explain that my friend is a level-headed professional who isn't prone to wild imaginings or fanciful speculation. Several medical tests were performed on this child, she explained. He had no brain tumour or sign of epilepsy, no mineral deficiencies or evidence of poisoning, and blood tests were normal. Test after test revealed no reason for his unusual behaviour, and my friend wondered whether the problem was spiritual in nature rather than physical.

Surprisingly, the medical doctors must have agreed because the final diagnosis on the young patient's chart was "possession." As a last-ditch attempt to help the youngster, his family asked their minister to perform an exorcism and say healing prayers. "The child was cured, and returned home," my friend said.

Although not every expert on the subject of exorcisms would support Larson's style of casting out evil, authorities from many cultures and Christian denominations take demon possession seriously, and their efforts, like those finally taken in this story, have been successful.

In an April 20, 2012, article, Bishop Don Bolen, of the Catholic Diocese of Saskatoon, told *Calgary Sun* reporter Michael Wood that Christian scripture describes Jesus' work in rebuking demons, but the church also looks "to psychology and to medicine to bring healing to the complicated things that go on in the human mind…." The article goes on to stress the importance of discerning "between mental health–related cases and those that may be real-deal Devil tampering."

The Catholic Church takes a more private approach to performing exorcisms than pastors like Larson do, especially if that kind of spiritual intervention occurs during a regular church service. Furthermore, authorities from various Christian denominations might not agree with each other about what defines "demon possession." Some practicing Christians might believe in angels, or may hold to the idea that the appearance of a ghost suggests the spirit of a deceased individual is asking for intercession, though individuals with this mind set would not automatically believe every case involving such phenomenon is demonic.

And though they don't perform exorcisms, secular organizations such as The Alberta Paranormal Investigators Society (TAPIS) based in Edmonton have explored the subject of demon possession. Although they are open to discussing a client's concerns in this area, TAPIS echoes the sentiments of other authorities in stressing the importance of conducting a thorough physical examination before exploring supernatural causes for unusual behaviour. When all other possibilities have been ruled out, then perhaps that is the time to look to the spiritual realm for answers.

Ghost Tours

If you've never had the pleasure of a personal brush with a ghost, but would like to know more about the subject, consider taking in a series of walking tours that point out some of Edmonton's more popular hauntings in the Old Strathcona district.

Edmonton Ghost Tours offers patrons local history lessons peppered with juicy helpings of hitherto unexplained stories such as the "little boy at The Rutherford House [and] the scientist who is still seen walking the halls of the Power Plant" at the University of Alberta, as the group's website explains. Calgary Ghost Tours offers a similar "spine-tingling" experience as well.

And if you have encountered the unexplainable and want a better insight into the meaning behind your experience, paranormal investigators such as Edmonton's Paranormal Explorers and the Calgary Association of Paranormal Investigators, offer a variety of services. One word of caution: before securing the services of any such organization, check out their background and their policies. The paranormal groups that pride themselves in their professional behaviour require their investigators to undergo a criminal record check, and new clients can be provided with endorsements on their work. Be wary of offers of help from those without such credentials.

Apparitions. Ghosts. Unexplained orbs appearing in photos. Are they real or imagined, or merely an emotional response to a physical stimulus like "a bit of undigested beef" as Ebenezer suggested? Are the people who claim to have witnessed the unexplainable, or experienced something that they think could only be from another realm, con artists or delusional? Or is it possible that the unsettled souls of those who have gone before us are reaching out, from time to time, for any number of reasons?

Psychic Chip Coffey has his own answer to these questions. He says, "Our souls make eternal connections."

With that view in mind, it's surprising that more ghost stories aren't circulating throughout the province.

Or maybe there are, but the witnesses involved are too scared to come forward.

Chapter Three

Examining the Unexplained and Otherworldly Phenomena

~

Reported sightings of unidentified flying objects in 2012 were up 100 percent from 2011, according to the 2012 Canadian UFO Survey, released by Ufology Research on May 12, 2013. A total of 1981 reports, an average of five reports for every day of the year, came in to the Winnipeg-based organization founded by Chris Rutkowski. And of those reports cited, 7.5 percent were "judged as unexplained."

"The number of cases in 2012 completely eclipses the previous record for the highest number of reports in one year, when 1004 reports were received in 2008," researchers stated in the 2012 survey. The document goes on to suggest that public awareness about agencies such as Ufology Research, which track and investigate UFO sightings, might be one factor in explaining the higher number of reports. Another explanation could simply be the "increase in the number of Chinese lanterns set aloft during celebrations in 2012."

Regardless of the reasons, here in Alberta, a three-fold increase in reports occurred in 2012; Ufology Research recorded 323 unexplained sightings compared with 101 in 2011. Sightings are rated on their reliability and their strangeness; the higher the sighting rates in these categories, the more interesting the case. In a footnote to this most recent survey, researchers listed 13 reports that made the "most interesting" list for 2012. Unfortunately, an Alberta sighting wasn't on that list.

But that doesn't mean the province hasn't made the grade when it comes to strange occurrences and unexplained encounters in previous years, such as crop circles, which are frequently attributed to impressions made by extra-terrestrial space ships.

~

As recently as the 1960s, the study of unidentified flying objects was taken seriously, and our government officials didn't rely on private researchers like the dedicated members of Ufology Research to carry the load of tracking, examining and monitoring UFO reports. A branch of the Department of National Defence was responsible for this job, and they had a specific protocol for handling incoming reports.

When the Canadian Forces headquarters in Ottawa received a report of a UFO sighting from civilians or police authorities, it was sorted into one of two main categories: either the information received suggested the viewer may have witnessed a fireball or meteorite, or the witness description didn't conform to the patterns associated with those natural phenomena.

From there, reports were further divided into one of three categories: the situation warranted a formal investigation; it was interesting but did not warrant an investigation; or it was uninteresting and did not warrant an investigation. Between January 1 and November 30, 1967, 190 UFO reports were filed in Canada. Of those, only nine were considered interesting and worthy of investigation.

This time an Albertan sighting made the cut.

Ken Patrige, a reporter with the *Camrose Canadian*, wrote about an interesting phenomenon that occurred in Duhamel, Alberta. Circular impressions—nicknamed the "What'sit" circles in the newspaper story following their discovery—were reported on Edgar Schielke's farm about 20 kilometres southwest of Camrose, on the morning of Saturday, August 5, 1967.

Schielke's cows hadn't returned from pasture on the evening of August 4. By the time he noticed, it was raining heavily, and the farmer decided to round them up the following morning. When Schielke arrived at the pasture the next day, he noticed "four circular marks approximately 30 feet [9 metres] in diameter." There were other markings too; Patrige wrote about seven in total in the August 9 edition of the local newspaper.

Schielke was fascinated with the discovery but didn't report it to the authorities. Still, the find was so intriguing that he told one of his neighbours about it. That unnamed neighbour shared the story with a local UFO enthusiast named Ray Saunders, and there was no turning back. The media soon got wind of the circles, along with special interest groups and the authorities with the National Research Council (NRC) in Ottawa. Schielke might have wanted to keep his discovery quiet, but as news of the circles spread, and officials from the Canadian Forces headquarters began to show interest, Schielke's pasture turned into a multi-ringed circus.

Officials Arrive on Site

A week after Schielke's discovery, Dr. G.H. Jones arrived from the Defence Research Establishment Experimental Station (DRES) in Suffield to investigate the matter in an official capacity. The pasture had attracted a lot of attention from the locals, so the site was far from fresh by that point. Jones said that Schielke was cooperative, but Jones admitted that the situation was hard to assess—did the farmer really want all that attention, or was he being honest when he appeared unconcerned about the circles and the interest the military, or anyone else for that matter, was taking in the situation? Jones couldn't be sure. But he didn't deny that the circles were odd, and he couldn't determine a definite cause for them.

After measuring each of the circular impressions, examining the clockwise appearance of the pressed grass, taking soil samples and interviewing residents about the rash of UFO sightings in the area, Jones documented his findings:

My conclusions from this rather quick investigation are:

The possibility of a hoax can be neither confirmed nor denied.

The marks in the ground could have been produced by a wheel in rolling contact, but this wheel would probably require a load of at least half a ton and the wheel would have to be moved in a rather exact circle.

The marks could have been produced by a vehicle sitting on a circular base—possibly flexible, provided the vehicle weighed at least 100 tons and possibly nearer 200 tons.

By the end of the summer, the furor over Schielke's mysterious crop circles had died down somewhat. No definitive cause of the impressions was ever discovered. The incident became one of those unsolved mysteries of local lore that parents tell their children about year after year and that keeps residents looking to the skies—especially on those nights when their cows don't make it home.

Extraterrestrial Footprints

The Duhamel episode wasn't a solitary event when it comes to the history of mysterious crop circles suddenly appearing in this province. A story in the August 30, 1991, edition of the *Edmonton Journal* told about four circles ranging from 5 to 7 metres in diameter that had been identified on a Lethbridge-area wheat farm. A week later, another crop circle was discovered in an Okotoks barley field. This one measured 17 metres in diameter. Both sets of circles could be seen by passing motorists, making it easy for curious onlookers to stop for a look and for skeptics to doubt they were formed by UFOs.

Less than a week later, four additional circles were discovered at two other locations. And while some non-believers held fast to the theory that someone was having a lot of fun at the public's expense, some residents were growing increasingly uneasy with the situation.

"It makes me nervous," farmer Jenny Skinner told reporters. "I don't think I want to be alone out here at night any more. We've farmed this land since 1960 and we've never seen anything like this."

The September 16 edition of the *Edmonton Journal* contained a story explaining how computer consultant Rob Day created a three-metre circle in 15 minutes with nothing more than a plank and a piece of rope. He confirmed what the naysayers believed all along—the southern Alberta crop circles were nothing but a hoax, after all.

Rob Day might have solved the 1991 mystery, but other occurrences of crop circles were a lot more difficult to debunk.

In 2002, the television program *Unsolved Mysteries* documented the case of a geometric pattern of seven crop circles of various sizes discovered by two farmhands in 1999 near Edmonton. The circles were initially dismissed as a hoax, and the local media didn't take even a cursory notice of the report of a 57-metre-long impression on the farm field where Rusty Manuel and Thelley Whitman worked. But when the non-profit

organization BLT Research Team Inc. of Cambridge, Massa-
chusetts, examined crop and soil samples from the site and
determined that the pattern couldn't possibly have been made
by hoaxers, *Unsolved Mysteries* finally took notice; they were
especially interested in the research results.

According to BLT Research, the crop damaged by a crop
circle has to be examined from a microscopic perspective to look
for "node elongation, expulsion cavities at the nodes, and germi-
nation abnormalities." If each of these conditions are noted in the
crop sample, it means the impressions weren't created by humans.

Atmospheric conditions at the time were also taken into
consideration during the investigation. Researcher and author
Colin Andrews (an electrical engineer turned UFO sleuth) told
Unsolved Mysteries, "We looked at meteorology. We looked at
earth energies. We looked at chemical application of the farm-
ers, and all of them led to a blank. It just did not fit. What we
now know is we have a solid mystery."

As a volunteer with the Canadian Crop Circle Research
Network, Alberta-based researcher Judy Arndt also took an
interest in the 1999 discovery. She spoke with the police officer
who'd been called to the site, and she also took photographs
and measurements. She made a detailed examination of the
location, noting every anomaly right down to what could have
been gopher holes. In addition, Arndt noted that when one
investigator was standing in the centre of the large circle at the
time, he couldn't use his cellphone. "The phone wouldn't work
and the battery power dropped rapidly by three points," Arndt
wrote, suggesting that perhaps the atmosphere was somehow

affected by whatever created the circle. "After being outside the formation for about five minutes, he was able to use his cellphone again."

Arndt assisted the authorities in the arduous task of collecting samples for BLT Research from the nettle-infested field. When addressing the suggestion that the circles may have been a hoax, she said, "If anyone wanted to hoax a formation, it's a puzzle to me why they would choose a field of prickly barley and thorny thistle. It's no place for a party!"

The crop circles were unquestionably a mystery in 1999, and they continue to defy explanation to this day.

Close Encounters of the First and Second Kind

Crop circles aren't the only unexplained phenomena that fall under the category of the unexplained. Flashes of light in the night sky, sudden explosive balls of fire, multicoloured lights and oddly shaped objects are just a few of the strange sightings that have been reported by witnesses throughout Alberta. Research organizations like to group sightings. Ufology Research, for example, divides sightings into four main designations: close encounters of the first, second, third and fourth kind, each of which describe various degrees of contact. First and second level encounters, for example, mainly focus on sightings of discs seen at night or during the day; the sightings may or may not include additional physical effects, such as blinking lights and fireballs in the sky. Close encounters of the third kind include sightings of what appear to be alien creatures, and encounters of the fourth kind include some type of physical contact, which may or may not include abduction.

Dateline: Nanton, 1967

Just before the unexplained crop circles appeared in Duhamel in August 1967, Warren Smith of Calgary was prospecting with two other men about 48 kilometres west of Nanton when he noticed something hovering just above the tree line in front of him. According to the report on file with the National Research Council (NRC) of Canada, Smith described the object as "circular, shiny, aluminum and approximately 25-feet in diameter" and said that it was hovering at an estimated 2000 to 2500 feet. It appeared to remain stationary long enough for Smith to snap two photographs before it descended somewhat, then darted behind some trees. Copies of the photographs were eventually sent to the University of Colorado, where UFO studies were being conducted. I could find nothing on file to suggest any conclusions in the matter were reached, leaving Smith with two shiny photographs and a mystery to share.

Dateline: Boyle, 1976

A reliable witness with a solid public image is always an important consideration when evaluating the dependability of an informant. So when on December 15, 1976, Boyle resident Arnold Barker, a well-known and respected member of the community, reported seeing a UFO while on his way to work at about 7:30 that morning, the members of his local RCMP detachment took it seriously enough to forward his report to the National Research Council.

In a four-page, handwritten statement, Barker said that he was driving "south on highway 46 two and three quarter miles north of Boyle" when he spotted two bright lights that looked to be about a half a mile away. "I thought this was unusual for an airplane because of the type of light," Barker wrote, giving a detailed description of the object's location in relation to his vehicle. Barker drove until the object was so close to his truck that he could no longer see it through the passenger window.

At that point Barker stopped his truck and got out so he could better see the two white lights. One appeared to be in front of the other, but he estimated they were each about two feet by four feet in size. The object was definitely flying, but it wasn't a plane. And when it got close to Barker's truck, the man did the unthinkable:

> I jumped out of the truck so that I could get a better look at it as it passed over head and across the highway. By this time there were no white lights…but two red lights, side by side four feet apart and not flashing. Each red light was in sort of a zig-zag pattern….

A lot was going on, but Barker said there was silence amid the visual commotion. For a moment he thought the object might land, and because it was so still he kept moving towards it. But before he got as close as he would have liked to, the object darted north.

Barker rushed back to his truck and continued to give chase. He was definitely going to be late for work, but he was the kind of man who didn't like a mystery he couldn't solve. Unfortunately, he had to satisfy himself with reporting what he saw, detailed diagrams and all, but without a satisfying conclusion. Once again, Alberta skies produced an unidentified flying object of the most mysterious kind.

Dateline: Berwyn, 1981

A few years later, the local RCMP detachment told Mrs. Jessie Kinley of Berwyn she should write to the National Research Council (NRC) after she saw something she couldn't explain. Located about 35 kilometres west of Peace River, Berwyn has a population of about 500 people. In her letter to the NRC, Kinley described herself as a 50-year-old educated woman who taught school for four years and enjoyed the study of nature in her spare time.

It was her attraction to the natural world that had her stargazing from her kitchen window at around midnight on February 17, 1981. Looking to the western horizon, she noticed a "bright pulsating light which appeared about three times as large as the planet Venus does when it is low in the sky as the morning or evening star." What appeared to be red, blue and green lights flashed in sequence, but the predominant colour was white, she explained. She watched the light for about 10 minutes before it finally disappeared.

Kinley explained that her children were in bed and her husband was in the bath, so no one else in the family could corroborate her story. However, the next morning, Kinley telephoned her friends to see if they'd witnessed anything that night. Gordon and Margaret Allan lived on a farm in the general vicinity where Kinley saw the flashing lights. Kinley was thrilled to find out that her friends had indeed witnessed something strange. Sometime between 8:00 and 10:00 that evening, Gordon, a pilot, had noticed a bright red light while he was walking across his yard. He could see the light clearly, despite the cloud cover. Schooled in meteorology, Gordon told Kinley that he didn't believe what they saw was a meteor nor, in his opinion, could it have been a plane. As far as Gordon was concerned, it was something he couldn't explain and, therefore, was an unidentified flying object.

Satisfied that she'd seen something, Kinley took her sleuthing a step further and contacted the Flight Service Station of Transport Canada at the Peace River Airport to see if there were any flights or other possible explanations associated with the airport for the lights. She was told that what she'd seen couldn't have been an aircraft. Furthermore, Kinley shared her story with other locals and learned that similar sightings were reported years before: the National Research Council has several reports on file of unidentified lights in the skies over the community of Berwyn and its surrounding farmland.

The National Research Council received Kinley's letter and kept it on file, adding to the annals of Alberta's mysterious sightings.

Animal Mutilations

Close encounters of the third and fourth kind often include experiences in which "figures or entities are encountered" or "an alleged abduction or contact experience" occurs. A look at Alberta's rural community provides some cases where an actual, alien encounter may have been responsible for several grisly finds.

Reports of alien encounters and UFOs were at a particular high in 1967. So when communities across Canada were considering ways to celebrate the country's 100th birthday, St. Paul responded with a proposal to build a UFO landing pad. What was quickly called the world's first UFO landing pad would later form a walkway to an adjacent UFO replica, which now doubles as the town's tourist information centre. The final touch to the UFO theme was a toll-free hotline manned by the Chamber of Commerce that encouraged residents to report any strange sightings. Over the years it has proved to be a well-used hotline.

The "dial-a-sighting" opportunity has ensured that unexplained stories similar to those listed earlier in this book are documented; if someone notices something out of the ordinary, they are more inclined to call it in. But a call into the UFO hotline in the mid-1990s unveiled a discovery far more gruesome than typical flashing lights in the sky. The caller reported that a dead cow had been mutilated. As luck would have it, the community had an expert on such occurrences.

St. Paul farmer Fern Belzil was an expert in animal mutilations—probably the only one in his field in this country.

Although animal mutation wasn't an area of expertise he'd aspired to, he had more experience in the subject than anyone else in Canada, and he'd been called out to investigate several such cases in the past.

Reports of animal mutilations date back to the late 19th-century England, but the first on this continent didn't appear until 1967, when a U.S. report of a horse mutilation caught the media's attention. It's unclear when Canada's first case of animal mutation was reported, but at least three occurred in the 1990s: one in Leduc on July 17, 1992, and two in St. Paul in 1999 (one on June 6 and the other on October 29). And a headline from the annals of a Lethbridge paper in 1979 announced: "Fifth Animal Mutilation in South Being Investigated—Suspect a Satanic Cult."

Unfortunately, animal mutilation cases have continued to keep Belzil busy over the years. On June 15, 2005, the *Lloydminster Meridian Booster* reported that Belzil had been called out to examine a 10-year-old cow discovered in a farmer's field 65 kilometres north of Lloydminster and just east of the Alberta-Saskatchewan border. Similar to other cases Belzil had been involved with up to that time, this cow's reproductive organs had been removed, along with its udder, one eye and an ear.

According to the article, very little blood was found at the scene, no footprints or tire tracks indicated an intruder had been on the premises, the incisions were expertly done and all of the farmer's other cattle had dispersed.

Sixty-eight-year-old Ray Riguidel had farmed all his life but had never seen anything like this before. When news of the farmer's cow circulated throughout the rural community, he was surprised to hear that rancher George Larre, who farms between Riguidel's ranch and Lloydminster, had had a similar experience years earlier.

"If you haven't seen it, I wouldn't expect anyone to believe it," Larre told reporter Kirk Sibbald. "But if you really see one for yourself, and you understand what coyotes will do, you know it's not predators."

Belzil maintains a website chronicling some of the mutilations he has investigated. Although cows make up the bulk of Belzil's investigations, he has also reported on the mutilation of a young lamb and a bull elk. Aside from St. Paul, other animal mutilations in Alberta have occurred in Cereal in 2000, St. Vincent in 2001, Veteran in 2002 and Derwent in 2003.

In all these cases, animal predators were ruled out as the cause of the mutilations. And although some investigators have suggested a satanic cult might have been responsible for at least some of the cases, without any footprints, tire tracks or other evidence, that claim would be impossible to substantiate. Nothing earthly seems to be responsible for the strange animal deaths, but the suggestion of extraterrestrial involvement has been bandied about in some circles, placing these stories into the annals of Alberta's UFO history.

UFO Landing Strip

On June 3, 1967, Paul Hellyer, Minister of National Defence, officially christened the landing pad at St. Paul and declared the town the Centennial Capital of Canada. A plaque beside the structure reads:

> *The area under the World's First UFO Landing Pad was designated international by the Town of St. Paul as a symbol of our faith that mankind will maintain the outer universe free from national wars and strife. That future travel in space will be safe for all intergalactic beings, all visitors from earth or otherwise are welcome to this territory and to the Town of St. Paul.*

Communities across the country were building their own centennial projects, and celebrating this milestone in Canadian history helped to knit Canadians together, forming a unique cultural fabric.

During the celebrations surrounding St. Paul's UFO pad, residents would learn that a similar landing pad already existed in Alberta—at the Canadian Forces Base (CFB) in Suffield. The landing pad in Suffield had been built in anticipation of someday welcoming extraterrestrial travellers, Hellyer was reported to have said to the St. Paul audience.

It is widely known that CFB Suffield was the chosen site for government chemical and biological weapons testing, but prior to Hellyer's announcement that day in 1967, officials never admitted to having a landing pad in Suffield. Some ufologists believe that the landing pad did exist at Suffield, and maybe still does.

The story goes that Wilbert Smith, Canada's leading cold-war UFO researcher from the 1950s, had a hand in encouraging the Canadian government to build the landing strip. Smith, a senior radio engineer with Canada's Department of Communications, was the mastermind behind Project Magnet at the Shirley's Bay Ontario research site. In that project, Smith studied geomagnetism, and he theorized that one might be able to "use and manipulate the Earth's magnetic field as a propulsion method for vehicles." He further argued that if astronauts from other planets were indeed visiting earth, perhaps these UFOs were recharging their batteries, as it were, during their flights over earth. "I feel that the correlation between our basic theory and the available information on saucers check too closely to be mere coincidence," Smith wrote in a report to the Department of Transport.

Smith managed to obtain public funding for his research, which included a side project that was "solely dedicated to dealing with 'flying saucer' reports." This much is public knowledge and is chronicled at the Library and Archives Canada's website dedicated to UFO reports throughout the years.

The twist in this story comes when some sources suggested Smith was also a proponent for Suffield's supposed UFO landing pad. An *Ottawa Journal* article from July 1967 reported that "The Canadian Government 13 years ago made available the defence research board experimental station at Suffield, Alberta, as a landing site for Unidentified Flying Objects."

It's interesting to note that the official making that statement was the same official who celebrated the opening of the St. Paul UFO landing site, defence minister Paul Hellyer. Hellyer's files on the matter were reportedly lost since that time.

Furthermore, UFO researcher Grant Cameron interviewed Smith's widow in 1978, asking her if she knew anything about a UFO landing pad. Mrs. Smith explained that her husband had indeed approached his superiors, explaining how a UFO landing pad would encourage aliens to meet with us face to face. The story goes on to suggest that Smith had conversed with "AFFA," a commander of a spaceship thought to be orbiting the earth in April 1954, and that AFFA would agree to land and meet with Smith's government if they were promised the freedom to take off again when they wanted to. Smith relayed this information to his superiors, but they wouldn't agree to AFFA's conditions.

Does CFB Suffield monitor a top-secret UFO strip at its base? Perhaps an even better question to ask is whether a UFO has ever landed there?

Chances are the Canadian public may never know the truth behind this story, and it too, like the many other sightings that have perplexed and intrigued investigators, will forever remain a mystery.

THE GEOGRAPHY
OF ALBERTA

Chapter Four

A Picture in Stone:
The Badlands Guardian

~

It was only the second time 53-year-old Lynn Hickox logged on to Google Earth, and she was even more exited than she had been the first time. She powered up her computer, logged on to the website that gave her a bird's-eye view of magnificent locations the world over and keyed in her username: "Supergranny."

Google Earth promises its users a "virtual journey to any location in the world." From the quaint, rural community of Gravelbourg, Saskatchewan, population 1200, where she lived, Lynn could travel almost anywhere her heart desired from the comfort of her own home. Today's goal: directions to Drumheller—her grandson, a dinosaur fan, wanted to see the Royal Tyrrell Museum, and maybe discover one or two fossils of his own.

Lynn had a general idea of where Drumheller was located, so she started scanning the rocky landscape to get a better feel for the overall geography. Moments into her search, something caught Lynn's eye. Did she just see what she thought she'd seen? She blinked and looked again. Yes, she hadn't imagined it. What Lynn was looking at appeared to be the image of a Native chief's profile, complete with feathered headdress, carved into the southern Alberta landscape.

~

Medicine Hat is in the southeastern quarter of the province along the South Saskatchewan River Valley and the TransCanada Highway. Labelling itself as "a community of choice," the city has drawn more than 61,000 residents with its beautiful scenery, abundant wildlife and rich natural resources.

But beauty isn't all Alberta's sixth largest city can offer its residents. The land surrounding Medicine Hat is perfect for ranching and traditional farming. As well, early on in the city's history, the drilling of a well extracted more than just drinking water. The quest for H_2O resulted in the discovery of one of the "largest gas fields in North America." Today, that gas field offers longtime residents and newcomers alike the means to make a good living.

Legendary Name

Historically, the lands surrounding Medicine Hat and throughout Cypress County served as the traditional hunting ground to members of the Blackfoot, Cree and Assiniboine nations. Their way of life was as much a part of the cultural landscape as their rich First Nations lore. Indigenous traditions have provided several stories explaining the reason behind the naming of Medicine Hat, but the city adopted the Blackfoot legend as the official story behind its name.

Etched on a brick mural at Medicine Hat's City Hall, and chronicled on the city's website, this legend tells of a terrible winter of famine that threatened to wipe out the Blackfoot nation. The young, the sick and the elderly were the first to succumb to starvation, but the strongest of the tribe would also die out if something wasn't done to rectify the situation.

According to the legend, a young man of the Blood tribe accompanied by his wife and his favourite wolf-dog were sent to a location called the "breathing hole." The breathing hole "on the river between what is now Police Point and Strathcona Park in Medicine Hat" was a sacred place to the Blackfoot people because they believed the "water spirits came up to breathe." Even in the dead of winter, when the rest of the water turns thick with ice, a misty fog is expelled through a hole in the glassy surface, as if someone—or something—were breathing up from the dark waters and into the cold air.

On arriving at the site, the young warrior and his new wife set up camp and began to call out the spirits. The story tells of how "a giant serpent rose from the misty waters" and promised to give the young Blood a "Saamis, or holy bonnet"— a "Saamis" is a headdress made from eagle tail feathers traditionally worn by a medicine man. This headdress would bless the young man with the ability to save his people from starvation with "special powers and great hunting prowess."

But the offer came with a price. In exchange for these gifts, the serpent demanded the man throw his wife into the river as a sacrifice. Not too happy with the proposition, the warrior threw his dog into the water instead. But the serpent spirit was not so easily appeased. He wanted the woman—nothing less would do. And so the heartbroken warrior reluctantly tossed his wife into the icy waters and, as directed, spent a lonely night on the nearby island of Strathcona.

"When the sun lights the cutbanks, go to the base of the great cliffs and there you will find your Medicine Hat," the serpent spirit instructed.

The cost was high, but with the magic of the Saamis, the "young hunter located the much needed game, saved his people, and eventually became a great Medicine Man."

And so it was that the tent town—which eventually sprang up along the South Saskatchewan River when the Canadian Pacific Railway built a bridge over the river—came to be known as Medicine Hat.

The story made for an interesting bit of Canadiana, but it was about to become much more interesting after a Google Earth discovery by the "Supergranny" from Saskatchewan.

Meanwhile, Back at Google Earth

When Lynn Hickox placed the coordinates of her satellite discovery on the Google Earth forum, she had no idea that her discovery of a chief's portrait moulded in stone would cause such a furor. At first she wasn't 100 percent sure if the unique site she found had already been charted by others. But she'd seen how other Google Earth users had pinpointed locations of geographic interest with a pin alongside their user names, and she thought she'd follow suit. She didn't wait around to see if anyone commented on it.

It would be months before she found out just how unique a find she had made.

Located at 50°0'38.20" N 110°6'48.32" W, the 255-metre by 225-metre geomorphological feature now known as the "Badlands Guardian" isn't something you can see without a satellite view. Even with the aid of a satellite, conditions have to be nearly perfect to see the image Lynn saw that November day in 2006. The light has to be "right to catch the shadow to sort of outline the face," Duane Froese, geology professor at the University of Alberta, told the CBC in an interview shortly after Hickox's discovery. For some, the geologist's description was connected to the serpent spirit's instructions to the Blackfoot about finding a "medicine hat." Hickox's discovery provided aerial viewers with information that would allow them to see the profile of a face to go with the headdress.

The stone is about 53 kilometres east of Medicine Hat, but the feature isn't discernable when approached from the ground; an aerial view is required. That's where Google Earth comes in.

Depending on how wide an angle you view the figure on Google Earth, you can almost imagine that the rocks surrounding the face look a little like wild horses in mid-gallop.

As evidenced by some of the chat room discussions about the Badlands Guardian, the mystical quality of the effigy has prompted several interpretations about the stone face, the land around it and the possible implication behind the images.

Ed Ziomek, a self-proclaimed "non-academic, amateur researcher studying ancient mythologies, ancient architectures, and ancient topographies," presents his own interpretations on his Flickr page. He said he could see two images in the satellite imagery from Google Earth: "the central King figure and an image of Pan, the God of the rising sun, fertility, and agricultural abundance." The mythology is of Mediterranean origin, but the photographs Ziomek shares offer an interesting comparison to the Badlands Guardian.

Scientist Steve Schimmrich, a geologist and community college professor from the mid-Hudson Valley of New York, provides a more academic view of the carved rock. "While neat to look at, this feature is simply an artifact of weathering and erosion, only seen from above under certain lighting conditions, and an example of something called *pareidolia*." Simply put, *pareidolia* is a psychological response to an image or sound that results in the viewer seeing "meaningful patterns or connections in random or meaningless data." Schimmrich likens the associations made between the Badlands Guardian and a chief's head to those made about the "face of the man on Mars." If challenged, perhaps Schimmrich may have compared it to the image of the Virgin Mary on a piece of burnt toast?

Undoubtedly, Schimmrich's view is less romantic than other theories.

From Humble Beginnings to Worldwide Fame

Lynn had no idea of the stir her discovery had made until she logged back onto Google Earth months later. That's when she found out that reporters from media outlets across Canada and as far away as Australia had tried to contact her. "At that stage nobody knew who I was," Lynn said, explaining that the only way of contacting her was through her Google Earth name, Supergranny. "It wasn't until after, when the CBC got a hold of me (after I responded to their email) that people knew I'd found the Guardian."

The media interest and the subsequent proposals that assigned a deeper meaning to the formation propelled a nation-wide search for a name of the wind-carved rock, courtesy of the CBC radio show *As It Happens*. According to one report, more than 50 names were submitted, but only seven were passed on to the Cypress County Council.

Among the first round of winning entries were The Listening Rock, Pod God, Az-tech, and iChief. These names specifically referred to the road running up the neck of the image and leading to an oil well, which was located right where the ear would be and gave the appearance that the traditional-looking warrior was wearing earbuds. In the end, the council altered their final selection slightly from the "Guardian of the Badlands" to "Badlands Guardian." And while council members may have enjoyed the process of naming the newfound mystic image in their midst, Stephen Hutcheon of the *Sydney Morning Herald* quoted county manager Lutz Perschon as saying that it was unlikely the Badlands Guardian would garner any kind of local tourism since the only road to the site isn't open to the public.

For Lynn Hickox, her Google Earth experience opened up endless possibilities of what could be found with the application. "You had all those explorers who had to traipse miles and miles, and here I am just sitting here at the computer with a mouse," she told CBC Radio.

No doubt there are thousands of yet-to-be discovered images around this planet we call home, and others like Hickox who will embrace the joy of discovery. But the Blackfoot people of southern Alberta would argue they didn't need a satellite to know that the "bump in the ground" we now call the Badlands Guardian existed. What was a newly uncovered, mysterious geological marvel to the rest of the world was as solidly embedded in the Blackfoot culture as the chiselled stone we now have the privilege of seeing with the help of modern technology.

One YouTube salute to the sacred image has made it quite clear that for the Blackfoot at least, there is no mystery involved. It suggests the Badlands Guardian is none other than the young Blackfoot-brave-turned-medicine-man who sacrificed all to save his nation and for whom the city of Medicine Hat is named.

"My people, the Blackfoot, always knew about this sacred place," the YouTube author says. Proof that the "Indigenous people have a strong connection to the land."

Chapter Five

The Badlands: Where the Past Meets the Present

A tour guide named Lena lines up all the children in my tour group.

"Let's pretend we are a large glacier, and we're moving in that direction," she tells them.

Arm and arm, with the guide in the middle, the children are instructed to shuffle their feet forward, dragging them on the ground as they cover a good 3 metres or so of the parched earth surrounding the Royal Tyrrell Museum.

"Stop," she says.

The children don't move, unsure of what comes next.

"Now, all together, let's shuffle our feet backwards."

Once they return to their original spot, the tour guide points out all the loose stones that were dragged across that 3 metres or so, and left behind when the children shuffled back.

"Those stones represent 'erratics,' rocks that are different from the kinds of rocks typically found in a particular geographic area," she explains, pointing to an example of a much larger erratic in front of us, which was left behind

when glacial ice receded from the valley that locals once referred to as "the ditch."

"That's how glacial ice moved these erratics from one place to another some 12,000 years ago—just like the way we shuffled our feet along the ground. And when the ice melted, those rocks were left behind where they fell. These erratics are one of the seven wonders of the Badlands."

As I look around at the canyons and ravines, the hoodoos and gullies, see the striations lining the hillsides harbouring layers of sandstone and clay and coal, it's apparent that the receding glaciers have left behind more than the erratics.

~

*I*ls sont des mauvaises terres a traverser.* ("They are bad lands to cross.")

That's what French explorers said when they traversed the otherwise gentle prairie lands leading up to a wide gorge of sandstone hills dominated by steep, brittle slopes and dotted with prickly pear cactus.

In 2005, Trevor Kiitokii, a spokesperson for Head-Smashed-in Buffalo Jump, told Yvonne Jeffery of the *Calgary Herald* that the "Badlands are looked at as one of the sacred places where the people, from my understanding, did not dwell, because it was the graveyard of the animals that lived there a long time ago. They knew that from stories from their ancestors…in the spiritual guidance, they were told this place was sacred."

This stretch of land is so unique that unless you've travelled through one of the world's few badlands locations, which are located in select regions of North and South America, New Zealand, Spain and, strangely enough, a corner of southern Taiwan, you'd be hard-pressed to understand Kiitokii's statement. The people he refers to are from Alberta's Blackfoot nation, which is comprised of the Kainaiwa (Blood), Piikani (Peigan) and Siksika (Blackfoot) tribes.

As with any world wonder, seeing is believing.

The Land Where Monsters Roamed

The Alberta Government website explains that of the 661,000 square kilometres of land in the province, the unique valley of sculpted hillsides boasting layers of sedimentary rock sandwiched between still more layers of softer clay and darkened coal seams that we call badlands extends from "Stettler in the north, through Drumheller and along the Red Deer River towards the southeast. The western border runs east of Red Deer, Calgary and Lethbridge. Saskatchewan and the U.S. border are the eastern and southern borders respectively." Dinosaur Provincial Park covers 50,242 square kilometres, occupying a considerable portion of the entire 90,000 square kilometres that make up all of the province's badlands.

One can only imagine what the first explorers to this province must have felt when they edged their way across the flat prairie grass and suddenly happened upon the sharp gorge that at times falls off without warning. What feat of nature caused such a sudden and drastic change to the environment? And why were these strange hills restricted to one particular section of an otherwise flat prairie?

Tourists of the Alberta Badlands that surround the small city of Drumheller can get an encapsulated view of the unique landforms carved through the earth by the abating glaciers and the 724-kilometre-long Red Deer River that continues to course along its winding path. Visitors can drive the 48-kilometre route known as the Dinosaur Trail, which just hints at what this magnificent landscape has to offer—a tip of icing on a teaspoon that, should anyone have the taste for it, only tempts the person to indulge in the entire dessert.

The mysteries entombed in these hills are in varying stages of discovery, but there are always more questions than answers when it comes to this corner of Alberta. Fresh discoveries are made every year as wind and water further erode these hillsides and as new fossil specimens are unearthed. And when subsequent explorers first traversed these hillsides in search of coal, easily located by the black seams separating layers of sedimentary rock, they made a discovery that would provide fodder for many more in the years to come.

Joseph Tyrrell was a 26-year-old geologist working for the Geological Survey of Canada and looking for coal on August 12, 1884, when he came face to face with a monstrous skull sticking out from a rock face not far from where his namesake, the Royal Tyrrell Museum, now stands. He wasn't the only man to have unearthed the remains of a dinosaur in the area; Canada's First Nations peoples were the first to discover the

massive skeletons they believed were the long-deceased ancestors of the bison that roamed the prairies and were a source of
food, clothing, weapons and warmth throughout the ages.

Tyrrell cautiously removed the skull, and it was eventually transported to Ottawa's National Museum of Natural Sci-
ences, where it landed in the hands of some of the world's top
scientists. And in 1905, the year Alberta became a province,
Henry Fairfield Osborn, a paleontologist with the American
Museum of Natural History in New York City, officially named
Tyrrell's find *Albertosaurus sarcophagus*, meaning "flesh-eating
lizard from Alberta." The Royal Tyrrell Museum later hailed the
geologist's finding as being "Canada's first known meat-eating
dinosaur."

Little did anyone at the time realize that Tyrrell's initial
find represented only a small tip of the iceberg. Paleontological
research in the Badlands continued to uncover more fossilized
giants, and it soon became apparent that establishing a museum
and research station would be prudent.

The Royal Tyrrell Museum first opened its doors in 1985
and received "Royal" status from Queen Elizabeth II in 1990.
Since then, the museum has upheld its mandate of "protection,
preservation and presentation of paleontological history, with an
emphasis on Alberta's rich fossil heritage." Scientists connected
with the museum are constantly on the hunt to uncover new
mysteries. And with fossils of at least 38 dinosaur species discovered in the Horseshoe Canyon formation of rocks alone,
researchers are rarely disappointed.

From Anonymity to World Heritage Site

So why is one of the most unique areas in Alberta the burial ground for so many different species of fossils?

"It was like the 'perfect storm' for making fossils," Royal Tyrrell museum science educator Joanna Northover said. "First of all, when the dinosaurs lived here, it was a lush environment with enough fresh water and plants to support them. At the same time it was a depositional environment, which means more sediments were being deposited than were being eroded."

Northover said that when the animals died, they were covered with the sand and mud washing down from the mountains forming to the West so "it was a good time to die and become a fossil."

Another contributing factor to their demise was the shallow ocean, known as the Western Interior Seaway, that covered Saskatchewan and Manitoba during the mid to late Cretaceous period. Massive storms of the magnitude of Hurricane Katrina blew in from time to time, flooding the landscape and killing the dinosaurs and other creatures. When the waters subsided, a layer of sediment and other debris blanketed the bodies, aiding the fossilization process.

As the Royal Tyrrell website states, "to early explorers, the badlands posed many challenges, but to palaeontologists, they hold the mysteries of ancient life." In 2010, the *Globe and Mail* reported that scientists discovered what many were calling the "largest dinosaur bonebed ever documented" near Hilda, in the southern portion of Alberta's badlands. The site opened up the possibility that horned dinosaurs lived in much larger herds than previously thought.

In 2012, the CBC reported on the discovery in August of a "2000-kilogram—or 4450 pound—triple-horned" triceratops just east of Drumheller. No doubt new discoveries will continue to captivate imaginations for generations to come because the question of what else is buried there remains a mystery.

For Alberta's First Nations peoples, the many bones littering the land suggested that the massive canyons, especially those passing through what is now Drumheller and into Dinosaur Provincial Park, were a graveyard where so many giants laid down for their final rest. Out of respect for the dead, the Blackfoot people often stayed away from the Badlands—some sources suggest First Nations peoples living in the area believed the dinosaur bones, like the hoodoos, "came alive at night to discourage intruders." But the dinosaur bones, and the supernatural activities associated with them, weren't the only reasons why indigenous peoples held the area in such high esteem. Another significant part of the landscape that echoed a reflection to the spirit world was the strange, stony structures we now refer to as the "hoodoos."

The Hoodoos

French explorers who first set their eyes on the unique rock formations had a considerably more fanciful name for these Badland sentinels; they dubbed them *chiminées de fée,* or "fairy chimneys." No doubt the travellers' country of origin influenced

The majestic stone sentinels known as the hoodoos have been formed by thousands of years of wind and water erosion. The French called the hoodoos *chiminées de fée*, or "fairy chimneys," reflecting on their ethereal nature.

how they perceived these natural wonders—"tent rock" and "earth pyramid" being two of the many monikers attached to these rocky pillars. But the name that most closely connected the land to the original culture of the area was the name "hoodoo."

It's uncertain exactly where the name "hoodoo" came from. Some sources credit the Europeans as the first people to refer to the mushroom-capped, rocky sentinels as hoodoos. Other scholars have suggested that the name "hoodoos" refers to the "voodoo" of African American traditions, a connection that mirrors the supernatural mysteries associated with both terms.

Still others, like Canadian author and broadcaster Bill Casselman, argue that any direct connection between the words "hoodoo" and "voodoo" is far from accurate, and there is little more than a "thin strand" of semantics that link the two words. He suggests that the word "hoodoo" is connected to "English-speaking fur trappers" who "used 'hoodoo' to refer to any malignant creature or evil supernatural force." Casselman's explanation makes sense when you consider that the Blackfoot people who roamed the Badlands both feared and respected these statuesque formations.

According to Joanna Northover, the Blackfoot people called the hoodoos "ma'tapiiks," which roughly translates to "the people." The Blackfoot people provide us with three interpretations of what these "petrified giants" may have represented: they were evil spirits trapped in rock; giants that came alive at night to "hurl rocks at intruders"; or spirits that protected the sacred lands. With these explanations in mind, a strong link can be made between the formations and their current popular name.

The most easily accessible and picturesque collection of hoodoos is located on Highway 10, about a 15-minute drive east of Drumheller. The rocks were formed during the Cretaceous Period, some 70 to 75 million years ago, and scientists estimate these geological structures were eroded by the wind and weather at a rate of about one centimetre per year. It took thousands of years to carve the majestic totems that capture the imaginations of tens of thousands of visitors every year. It's no wonder that the Royal Tyrrell Museum ranks the hoodoos as one of the seven wonders of the badlands.

The vast accumulation of sedimentary rocks, the plethora of fossils, the hoodoos and erratics, the petrified wood, the

The Blackfoot people referred to the hoodoos as "petrified giants."

Legend has it that horses would disappear into the striated hillsides of the Red Deer River valley's Horse Thief Canyon. When the horses finally reappeared, they would be wearing a different brand.

⁓

"popcorn rock," or bentonite clay, and the prickly pear cactus all add to nature's wonders that, until you see them, almost defies imagination.

Imaginative and inventive business-minded individuals have devised ways to unearth some of the mysteries of a bygone era for visitors to experience. The museum Fossil World, for example, has created a motion-activated scale model T-Rex. They call this mechanical monster the "finest animatronic dinosaur made in the world." If you visit this attraction, you'll most likely agree that standing underneath the monster makes you feel as though you're in the 3-D version of *Jurassic Park*.

If you're on the hunt to discover a new mystery or are content with revisiting solved ones, the Badlands promise something no other landscape can provide in quite the same way. And if you sit quietly on the hillsides of Horse Thief Canyon, where thieving cowboys were said to lasso horses and brand them as their own, you might just hear the whispers of another era, catch the vision of ancient wildlife and see the hoodoos hurl stones—and you'll disappear into a world long gone but, thankfully, not forgotten.

Chapter Six

The Mountain that Moves: The Frank Slide

~

It had felt like an unusually long day, and 15-year-old Lillian Clark was more than ready to go home.

Nothing felt better than sitting down to dinner surrounded by the chatter of her six younger siblings and Mom, taking care of her again. Lillian was old enough to work and contribute to the family coffers. It wouldn't be too long before she was old enough to marry, too. But for now, she was happy to be a daughter, ready to leave her tiresome chores at the local boarding house where she was employed and go home to the Clark family abode on Manitoba Avenue.

Lillian revelled in the fact that her mom, Amelia, was waiting for her, eager to make her first-born feel like her little girl for a bit longer. Lillian would tease her younger siblings, roll around on the floor and cause a general, happy mayhem before it was time for Mom to put the youngsters to bed. Lillian could forget about the world of work if only for the night. Yes, she was anxious to go home.

Weird how life has a way of surprising us just when we think we know where it's leading.

For reasons that seem forever lost to history, Lillian decided not to go home that night. She'd been working the late shift and was extremely tired. And although Amelia had never allowed Lillian to sleep at the boarding house, no matter how late or how exhausted Lillian might have been, Amelia relented that night. It was the first time Lillian had slept anywhere other than in her own bed. That night there would be no teasing her siblings, no ruffling her familiar bed pillows or pulling the comforter her mother spent months sewing for her up over her nose. Instead, the exhausted Lillian bedded down in the home of her employers.

She never imagined she wouldn't taste her mother's home cooking ever again.

~

One legend explains that in 1853, a battle between the Blackfoot and Crow peoples took place at the base of Turtle Mountain, located in southern Alberta's Crowsnest River Valley. Hundreds of warriors were killed when large rocks fell from the mountain peak during the battle, caused, it was believed, by the mountain having moved.

Perhaps this story was the foundation for another legend from both the Blackfoot and Ktunaxa cultures, which have long since referred to the rocky mound as "the mountain that moves." These indigenous peoples refused to camp near the base of Turtle Mountain because they thought the mountain might dislodge its monstrous boulders onto their campsites and destroy everything in its path.

Research at the Frank Slide Interpretive Centre suggests that the legend the indigenous peoples used to explain why the mountain moved quite likely had a basis in scientific fact:

Almost certainly, the prehistoric people who mined chert, or flint, across the valley as much as 5000 years ago and left pictographs near timberline on adjacent Bluff Mountain had traversed Turtle Mountain's crest, where it is

One can only imagine the horror onlookers must have felt as they helplessly watched the smouldering fire consume what remained of seven miners' cabins.

believed that they would have seen the massive cracks and fissures along the summit ridge. They may also have observed seasonal rockfalls.

"They would have seen big cracks, year after year, and maybe even noticed that the cracks got bigger," the centre's education officer, Joey Ambrosi, explained further.

Regardless the theory involved, Turtle Mountain—named by rancher Louis O. Garnett because he thought the mound, from a distance, looked like a turtle's shell—was about to make history.

~

In his book *Frank Slide*, J. William Kerr reports the First Nations legend surrounding Turtle Mountain was appended as recently as the night before the slide when it was rumoured that an "Indian Chief" warned the town's "mayor" to "move the people away because the mountain was about to fall." The chief in Kerr's account wasn't associated with any particular tribe in the area, and Frank, being a company town and a new community at that, most likely didn't have an official mayor at that time, but this part of the legend provides an interesting segue into what quickly became a tragic story.

It was 4:10 AM on April 29, 1903. Too early for local miners pulling the day shift to relieve the graveyard workers at the town's main employer, the Canadian American Coal and Coke Company. In a couple of hours, most of the residents in Frank would need to rouse themselves from their peaceful slumber.

The next few moments proved particularly fateful for the 90 or so residents still sleeping in their homes at the foot of Turtle Mountain that morning, as well as the 20 miners who just clocked off for their 4:00 AM meal break. By the time the underground workers recognized a movement or sound that was out of the norm for that time of day, the cataclysmic event known as the Frank Slide was already over. And any of the residents curled up in their beds who might have been awoken by the commotion wouldn't have had the chance to pull off their covers before they were crushed by a staggering 150 to 200 metres of rock and clay.

Based on reports from Frank residents living outside the slide zone, the avalanche that tumbled the 4 kilometres from the summit of Turtle Mountain took a mere 100 seconds to blanket an area on the valley floor roughly one kilometre wide and 1.5 kilometres high.

Boulders as large as houses blocked passage to the only road through town—to this day, many of those boulders remain where they fell. Seven cottages on the town's easternmost street, Manitoba Avenue, were either completely crushed or moved from their foundations and surrounded by rock. All of the mine's outbuildings, including the tipple (the "structure where coal [was] cleaned and loaded onto railroad cars"), were destroyed, along with a nearby construction camp, "a dairy farm, two ranches, a shoe store, a livery stable, the Frank cemetery, two kilometres of cart track, two kilometres of Canadian Pacific Railway line, and 1.5 kilometres of the just-completed Frank and Grassy Mountain Railway line." And the noise from the slide was so deafening, "like steam escaping under high

Smoke rising from the demolished cabins following the Frank Slide resembled, for some, the souls of the recently departed escaping their rocky confines.

pressure," that some residents of Cochrane, 200 kilometres away, reported hearing it.

Seeing Is Believing

Most of the residents in the untouched portion of town awoke to the shock of dust and debris clouding the sky, which must have looked like Armageddon to them. Jim Warrington thought the town had been hit by a violent hailstorm, only to find he'd been displaced from his home, covered in rock and suffering from a broken femur.

A half a kilometre away from the eastern edge of the slide, Karl Cornelianson heard a loud roar and thought the mine had exploded. When he looked out his bedroom window, he saw a wall of rock tumbling down with such force that it flung itself "upward on the north side of the valley" before falling back down again.

All the dust had settled when William M. Pearce, the chief inspector of surveys for the Department of the Interior, arrived at the scene the next day. He described what he saw to one news correspondent:

> *Disaster caused by* [a] *rock slide about four thousand feet long, extending from the extreme height of Turtle Mountain. The west end of the slide is about three hundred feet above the mouth of the mine tunnel. The slide extended out fan-shaped and crossed the valley and went up on the opposite hill about four hundred feet above the level of the valley. One and one quarter miles from the base of Turtle Mountain the river is totally obliterated for over a mile, and in some places covered by rocks one hundred and fifty feet deep...*

The reporter interjected at the end of Pearce's comments and said it was "an awful and grand sight looking at the scene of the disaster and the wreck. It must be seen to be realized."

The exact number of causalities was uncertain, since transient construction crews often camped out in the area. One report said such a crew had been there just days before the slide, and from a town of about 600 residents, an estimated 92 lives were lost. Among the dead were young Lillian Clark's parents and six siblings, buried in a tomb of rubble in their Manitoba Avenue home; Lillian's one night away from home saved her life, but she lost everything.

The death toll could have been much higher had it not been for the quick thinking of one man. The crew of a CPR freight train arrived at the Frank Station just moments before the slide hit the east side of town. The CPR workers knew that the passenger train, the Spokane Flyer, was on its way to Frank. In the darkness of the early morning, the engineer of the Spokane Flyer would not have been able to see the slide before it was too late and would have plowed into the pile of rubble blocking the track, causing certain death to all on board. Because the telegraph lines were down, and there was no way of warning the engineer, CPR brakeman Sid Choquette took it upon himself to race across the roughly 2 kilometres of boulder-ridden track to flag the Flyer down before it was too late. Miraculously, he arrived just in time to stop the train.

With few exceptions, most of the people in the slide's path died. Among the handful of survivors was 15-month-old Gladys Ennis. When her parents finally managed to free themselves and their three other children from their damaged Manitoba Avenue home, they saw Gladys' seemingly lifeless body slumped over a pile of mud and debris. Fearing the worst, the parents rushed to their baby's side to discover that her nose and throat were caked with mud. Thankfully, they were able to clear her airways and, aside from some minor injuries, baby Gladys survived.

Another toddler, 27-month-old Marion Leitch, was either thrown from her house to relative safety, ripped out of her dead mother's arms, or discovered in her family's attic after the slide hit her home, depending on the rendition of the story you choose to believe. Although no one really knows the details surrounding Marion's miraculous survival, theories abound. Unfortunately, Marion's story didn't have the same happy ending as Gladys'. Marion's parents were killed in their home, along with Marion's four brothers. Her two older sisters survived, however, and it is believed the three girls were raised by an uncle in nearby Cranbrook, BC.

The stories of Gladys and Marion seem to have provided the fodder for perhaps the most persistent legend surrounding the Frank Slide. Since that black April morning in 1903, a story has been repeated so many times that even people who know nothing else of Frank's history can tell of how Turtle Mountain spilled itself over the entire town one day, killing everyone in its wake except for one baby girl. The story is fictitious, and the baby girl, named by her unknown rescuers as "Frankie Slide," never existed. But perhaps the survival of two little girls from such a horrifying ordeal inspired hope in the hundreds upon hundreds of people who were mourning the loss of their loved ones in the aftermath of the Frank tragedy.

Buried Alive, But Safer Than Others

The most surprising story of survival comes from the 17 miners who were buried underground during the slide.

A crew of 20 was working the graveyard shift on the morning of April 29. Two of the workers had just brought a load of coal up to the tipple and decided to have their meal break with the weighman; the breath of fresh air was a nice treat in an otherwise underground job. Ironically, that break from the darkened coal mine was what claimed the lives of those three men.

The 17 other workers in the mine knew something was terribly wrong when the trembling earth knocked them off their feet, and a cold rush of air extinguished the lights they were carrying. Their first instinct was to escape out the mine's entrance, but as the workers converged from their various locations, they discovered the pathway to safety had been sealed by falling debris. Showing remarkable resolve, the workers didn't panic. Instead, they caught their breath and discussed their options. Digging through the rubble to get to the entrance seemed like the most obvious road to freedom. But after doing several calculations, they believed they'd have to dig anywhere from 15 to 90 metres—a seriously daunting task given that the men were already exhausted from the first half of their shift.

Scrambling for other alternatives, one group of three miners descended back into the mine to see if they could escape through one of the mine's other airways while a second group went to check out yet another tunnel. Both teams of men were devastated to find that both those options were considerably less promising than their first; water was pouring into the lower tunnel, obstructing the opening through that route, and coal gas was filling the blocked main tunnel. Digging their way to freedom was not only their best option, it was their only option.

The group reconvened and started digging. But the backbreaking work yielded almost no results. Feeling discouraged and defeated, the miners were fast losing hope, when one of the men remembered a coal seam that surfaced not far from the mine's now-blocked entrance. Digging through coal was easier than digging through what felt like cement-strength limestone, so the men agreed to give it a try. They had no idea how far they'd have to dig to reach the surface; the distance to the outside world might be longer than the one at the mine's entrance, but they were hoping they'd be more productive.

Working in shifts, groups of two or three men took turns picking their way to the surface. After 13 hours, the men had spent their reserves. Any air and energy they may have started

The landscape has remained so remarkably unchanged since the Frank Slide that visitors who are previously unaware of the town's history are often shocked it happened so long ago.

~

out with were now almost non-existent, and any shred of hope that remained was quickly fading away. And then Dan McKenzie's pick pierced through the last veil of earth separating the men from fresh air and freedom. One by one, the men pulled their tired bodies from the tunnel and hoisted themselves onto solid ground. The joy they must have felt turned sour when they witnessed the ruin around them. According to Kerr, the miners had successfully dug their way through "20 feet of coal and nine feet of limestone boulders" only to see that many of their homes had been buried under an even deeper layer of rock.

For William Warrington, surviving the ordeal with a broken leg wasn't the most challenging part of the night. William emerged from the rubble to discover his wife and six (or seven, sources disagree) children were not among the slide's survivors. His family members were among the 92 people thought to have been killed by the slide. Only 12 of the 92 bodies were recovered immediately after the disaster; another six bodies (believed to be members of the Clark family) were pulled from a home uncovered by a road construction crew in 1922.

Tragedy, Horror, Shock

"Earthquake almost destroyed town. Hundred killed. We are all safe." The dispatch was sent by a representative of P. Burns and Co., a meat-packing company, to their offices in Cranbrook. On orders from Patrick Burns, owner and founder of the company, aid was sent to Frank residents following the slide.

Explanations for why Turtle Mountain had dumped a load of limestone onto the valley floor centred around two possibilities: an earthquake had occurred and dislodged portions of the mountain, or an explosion in the coal mine had caused the rock slide. It was quickly determined that neither theory was correct, which left a very unsettling conundrum. What had caused the slide? And were the residents of Frank at risk of experiencing another, perhaps even greater, disaster?

Fear of another slide did not squelch human curiosity. Within days, news of the slide drew a steady stream of onlookers to the site. However, reactions from those living in the shadow of Turtle Mountain were considerably more diverse, ranging from an intense foreboding that the remainder of the hovering mountain would crash down and finish off the rest of the town, to the calm resolve required to pick up and get back to the routines of their lives. Some residents simply packed their bags and moved away, but most of the townsfolk stayed. Work began to stabilize, a makeshift road was built around the rubble and railway crews started clearing and rebuilding the destroyed track.

Meanwhile, Premier Frederick Haultain, after arriving at the site and learning that new fissures on the top of the mountain could mean the threat of another slide, initially ordered residents to leave town until scientists with the Geological Survey of Canada (GSC) declared the area safe. Although they noticed many concerns with the mountain's stability, geologists R.C. McConnell and R.W. Brock gave the all-clear, and residents returned to town by mid-May.

That said, research into the cause of the slide, and monitoring of the mountain, has continued to be an ongoing concern since 1903.

Theories Surrounding the Slide

Officials examining the disaster site at Frank originally blamed the coal mine, which ran horizontally for 2 kilometres inside the mountain, for the slide. Miners had already hauled out "more than a quarter of a million tons of coal" between 1901, when the mine opened for business, and 1903. Months before the slide, miners had noticed that the coal was falling on its own with increasing regularity; the miners had joked that "overnight the coal had mined itself."

The large timbers used to frame passageways within the mine and to "hold the roof up" showed signs of strain as large cracks often split the beams. And according to literature from the Frank Slide Interpretive Centre, "there were times, usually during the early morning hours, when the floor of the mine pitched as if it were a ship rocked by an ocean wave." The amount of coal pulled from the mountain's core might have eventually created a gap so large that the supporting timbers could no longer hold the weight of the remaining mountaintop.

Still, concerns that the mine had already threatened the stability of the mountain and that further mining would only continue to degrade its integrity didn't dissuade the Canadian American Coal and Coke Company from returning to business as usual. Families were still grieving their dead, and the altered

A sculpture of the Frank Slide created by Manitoba artist Michelle Elliott captures one of the biggest mysteries surrounding the Frank Slide—just how many people were buried alive?

landscape continued to cast a pall over residents, but the mine was re-opened for business just 31 days after the slide.

The question of mining aside, ongoing research into the mountain's geological stability raised several theories about what contributed to the slide:

> *The mountain's once horizontal layers of sedimentary rock had been folded during the mountain building process until almost vertical—the ultimate in mountain instability. A major thrust fault—the Turtle Mountain Thrust Fault— runs through the mountain. The thrust fault further divides and weakens the layers of rock within the mountain.*
>
> –Frank Slide Interpretive Centre website

Along with the vertically thrust layers of rock making up Turtle Mountain, water and ice seeping into cracks between the layers widened those gaps and further eroded the structure. Geologists suggested that a small cave near the summit of the South Peak, along with "a sulfur spring, which continues to 'eat' the mountain's foundation beneath the North Peak" also contributed to the mountain's instability.

Additionally, there were suggestions that softer layers of shale and clay at the mountain's base, along with the various coal seams, added to the mountain's top-heavy balance. This was especially true after an estimated 82 million metric tonnes of rock fell during the slide, altering the mountain's overall structure and splitting its peak into two distinct halves, which are now called the North Peak and South Peak. Eventually, the Geological Survey of Canada was so concerned about the stability of the North Peak that what remained of the town of Frank was moved to "New Frank," northwest of the original townsite. Today, scientists no longer expect the North Peak to fail, and industry and businesses have once again settled into Frank's original townsite.

Despite new confidence in the stability of the North Peak, ongoing studies of the mountain continue to monitor the geological movements in all parts of the mountain. The Alberta Geological Survey (AGS) took up the task of long-term monitoring of the mountain in 2005, installing a network of more than 80 sensors. Dr. John Allan, founder of AGS, is one scientist who still has concerns that the upper and lower South Peak as well as the lower Third Peak are vulnerable to a potential slide.

No one can really state, with any authority, the sole reason behind the Frank slide in 1903, nor can it can be foretold whether another similar disaster will occur and if so, when. Only time will tell if the mountain will once again offload some of its heavy limestone overhangs.

Today, more than 110 years after the slide, visitors to Frank can still see the devastation. "Year after year people visit and ask how the rock fell and missed the road and the railway track," Ambrosi said, explaining that for people who don't know the town's history, it looks like the slide occurred just recently. He explained that limestone, when it breaks down into soil, degrades the soil so it doesn't produce much, if any, vegetation. Therefore, the vast expanse of grey that covers the area to this day resembles a war zone.

For those people aware of the town's history, the stark landscape is a constant reminder of the devastation Mother Nature can unleash when she chooses to.

"There are still people in the Pass who lost family long ago, and for us, the people who live here, it's quite a spiritual place…" Monica Field, manager for the Frank Slide Interpretive Centre told Canadian Press reporters in 2012. "I have been along the railway tracks where the rows of miners cottages was hit, and it's a strange feeling to think you're right above the place where so many people died and they're still under there."

Alberta's Bermuda Triangle

Even today, the Frank Slide is renowned as the deadliest slide in Canadian history, and at the time it occurred, it was the largest. But it wasn't the only mining disaster the Crowsnest Pass region would see. On December 9, 1910, less than a decade after the slide, and only a kilometre away, an explosion at the West Canadian Collieries mine in what was then the community of Bellevue, claimed 31 lives. The mine workers were given a foreshadowing of the coming doom when an explosion occurred in the mine earlier that same year. That first explosion did not produce any fatalities.

Four years later, on June 19, 1914, another powerful explosion decimated the Hillcrest Mine, located just one kilometre southeast of Frank. Of the 250 men working that day, 235 were either mining coal or working on the underground tunnel structures when the explosion occurred. The tragedy claimed 189 lives; many of the miners succumbed to the deadly gases left behind by the fire. At least one of those dead miners, and possibly more, had been among the 17 survivors of the Frank Slide. Unlike the Frank Slide, the Bellevue and Hillcrest disasters were both believed to be the result of coal dust explosions.

Joey Ambrosi said the three disasters represent the three worst mining disasters in Alberta history. Occurring in such close proximity to one another, these tragedies have led locals, folklorists, historians and researchers alike to dub this corner of the province as "the little Bermuda Triangle of Alberta."

Regardless of the geology of the area and the scientific theories about why Turtle Mountain dumped part of its load on the town of Frank and the eerie coincidence tying three mining disasters into a mythical triangle, tourists still flock to the Crowsnest Pass region. They are drawn by the area's beauty and rich history, which is tinged with an aura of mystery. Some come to see how a whim of Mother Nature can forever alter a landscape. Others, aware of the legends surrounding the Frank Slide, visit the town out of curiosity while others embark on a treasure hunt in the hopes of unearthing the thousands of dollars that some suggest are buried beneath the rubble. Those of an investigative nature might be looking for answers about the identity of the chief who allegedly warned of the town's impending doom. Some visitors might stop by with trepidation, wondering if another portion of the mountain will eventually crash into the valley floor during their visit. Whatever their reason for visiting Frank, all visitors leave with a library of legends and a deeper understanding of one of this province's most mysterious geological disasters.

Chapter Seven

A Nugget of a Story: The Lost Lemon Mine

It had been a long and tiring day. Not even a whisper of a breeze moved the stagnant air, which was thick with the blackflies that had needled the miner's exposed skin all day.

The blistering heat added to the man's discomfort, and he paused for a moment to wipe the sweat from his brow. Were he to see a glint of promise in the granules of sand in his pan he would have been happy. As it was, the weeks had passed with little to no remuneration for his efforts; he was beyond discouraged. What would his wife have to say about his wanderlust when he finally made his way back to Edmonton? "Waste of time!" she'd say and, "How will we feed the babies over the winter?"

The sharp snap of a tree branch startled the weary miner and brought his thoughts back to matters requiring more immediate attention. The afternoon sun would soon be edging its way behind the neighbouring mountain, and he needed to make camp and prepare for the night. The sudden noise interrupting an otherwise silent scene also reminded him that at any moment he could move from the status of would-be miner to that of victim of the latest gold rush fever, which often attracted the less than honourable among his contemporary adventurers.

Desperadoes were known to frequent this area, looking to unearth some of the gold that was supposedly hidden up in the hills along the eastern slope of the Rocky Mountains. Others, a considerably more ruthless variety of bandit, wanted to rob any honest, hard-working prospector they might come across and make away with anything of value.

Suddenly, thoughts of home, his wife's stew and biscuits, her warm embrace and the giggles his little girls treated him to whenever they greeted him became a lot more appealing than discovering gold. They didn't need a life of ease; they just needed each other. They were already rich! Yes, he needed to go home.

Just one more day…or maybe two…he decided, and then he'd pack it up for the winter.

~

Gold. Commonly considered one of the most valuable and sought-after minerals ever discovered, gold has caused the rise and fall of many a man and nation. Lydian merchants turned gold into coins for use as currency as far back as 700 BC. Promises of gold-rich mountains lured explorers to North America from as early as 1540.

In 1799, Conrad Reed made what is widely considered the first gold discovery on this continent, in North Carolina. But it wasn't until 1828, when several claims of discovery were made in various locales of what is now the state of Georgia, that North America ushered in its first, official gold rush.

A steady stream of men from around the world descended on Georgia en masse in an effort to capture a piece of the mother lode. Carrying as little as possible—often just a pickaxe, a shovel, a pan and a bedroll—these young men would roam the streambeds and walk the Native packing trails in search of the elusive mineral.

The scene was replicated time and time again as one and then another gold discovery promised more opportunities—and an even bigger paycheque than the one before. Greed rapidly replaced the innate need to provide for one's family, and ruthlessness trumped honour in the hearts of many unsavoury characters.

According to *The Canadian Encyclopedia*, gold was first discovered in the vast expanse of the untamed wilderness north of the U.S. border in 1823 along the banks of the Chaudière River in the Eastern Townships of Québec. Another 30 years would pass before the great Cariboo Gold Rush got its kick-start with the discovery of the precious metal along British Columbia's Fraser River, drawing thousands of people across the border and into the promising mountainsides and creek beds of the BC interior. And in 1898, strikes farther north, in the Yukon, promised even greater wealth to anybody willing to brave the extreme cold and primitive living conditions of the backcountry.

Amid all the excitement, adventurous miners migrated off the main trails every now and again, testing out the road less travelled and looking for their own, private, strike.

In the spring of 1870, long before the promise of Yukon gold would have definitely drawn them farther north, two such miners, along with a handful of Métis guides, were said to have split off from a group of prospectors making their way from Tobacco Plains, a region that spanned the Canada and U.S. border between Montana and British Columbia, to the North Saskatchewan River.

The story that follows contains a potpourri of characters, plot points and details from several sources. Although many of these accounts share an overall theme, others differ in almost every aspect, from the names of the main players involved to the locales they explored and the claims they were said to have made. Perhaps it is because of these discrepancies that the legend of the Lost Lemon Mine that Albertans have come to know and love has withstood the test of time and continues to capture the imaginations of mystery lovers everywhere.

As Legend Has It

The two characters of dubious distinction said to have broken away from this particular expedition in the spring of 1870 and who were primarily responsible for the legend of the Lost Lemon Mine were known as Lemon and Blackjack.

One account suggests Lemon's name was Bill, while others called him Joe, Jack, Robert, Frank, Ben, James and Mark, or don't refer to a given name at all. Lemon purportedly stood about 5 feet, 10 inches in height, was of stocky build and could have been employed as a blacksmith prior to his wilderness wanderings. He may have hailed from Cedar Creek, Montana, before crossing the border and exploring the unmined territory of Canada's two westernmost provinces.

Blackjack was an equally enigmatic individual. D.E. Riley, the mayor of High River in 1906 who was also elected to the Senate in 1925, called Blackjack the "best prospector in the west" and the "real discoverer of the Caribou diggings in British Columbia" in what has become the most famous account of this story of discovery and intrigue. But discrepancies also exist around Blackjack's true identity. Well-known Alberta historian and author, Dr. Hugh Dempsey suggested that Blackjack was actually Nehemia (also spelled "Nehemiah") T. Smith of Maryland. Dempsey agreed with Riley's suggestion that Blackjack, caught up in the wave of the Fraser River Gold Rush of 1858, discovered gold in the Caribou, with his "most famous strike being in the Blackjack tunnel on William Creek in 1862." The problem with identifying the Blackjack of this story with that of the famed William Creek strike will be examined later, but it makes sense that Lemon would pair up with such a knowledgeable and experienced prospector when the two set out on their own.

Lemon's Diggings

Financially backed by Pennsylvania-born Lafayette French, a jack-of-all-trades trader and prospector who apparently accumulated some of his wealth as a former oilman,

Lemon and Blackjack had their eyes set on the lesser-explored lands of southern Alberta. Accompanied for a time by their Métis guides, headed by a man named La Nouse, Lemon and Blackjack wandered into what was widely believed at that time to be "hostile" Blackfoot territory. Carefully making their way south from High River back to Tobacco Plains, the pair prospected along an old First Nations pack trail beside mountainside streams and riverbeds and through the sporadic gravel deposits they happened upon. According to Riley's story, their efforts resulted in the discovery of "rich diggings from grassroots to bedrock."

Encouraged, the pair decided to explore a little deeper, digging two good-sized pits in the process. In the end, it wasn't their hard work that uncovered one of the purest finds of gold ever discovered along Alberta's foothills. Instead, Riley explains that as Lemon and Blackjack were bringing their cayuses (small horses used to carry mining gear) "in from the picket line, they accidentally discovered the ledge from which the gold came."

They'd discovered gold! Gleaming nuggets of pure gold with "little rock running through them." The find was so spectacular and so surprising that it set the two men at odds against one another.

Exactly what started the argument, and which man took which position, is unclear. But a war of words ensued that allegedly had to do with whether the men should set up camp and stake their find right then and there, or leave the area that would come to be known as "Lemon's Diggings" to return later in the spring.

With darkness creeping upon them, Lemon and Black-jack had to make camp for the night; at this point in the story, it appears the prospectors and their Métis guides had already parted company. Tired from the day's events, and emotionally spent because of the exhilaration of the find and the tension from their argument, the two men crawled into their respective bedrolls. They would make better sense of their situation in the morning—at least, that's what Blackjack might have thought.

Lemon, on the other hand, had other ideas.

Once Blackjack was fast asleep, legend has it that Lemon crept across the camp, picked up the axe that lay beside the prospectors' now-smouldering fire pit and thrust it down on the head of his sleeping partner.

The story goes on to explain that Lemon, stunned by the enormity of his actions, stood paralyzed with horror. Looking down on the split and bleeding head of the man whose expertise had helped lead them to their find, Lemon lost his mind. Crazed with an anxiety of his own making, Lemon walked back and forth around the campsite. He wanted to run, but to where? The night, made darker by the surrounding trees that threatened to suffocate him, left Lemon confused and disoriented. Heaping wood on the fire, in an almost desperate attempt to push away the blackness enveloping him, Lemon continued to pace throughout the night.

Although he tried not to look, he couldn't avoid seeing Blackjack lying there, still as death, on the bloodstained earth. And every once in a while he heard a moaning and groaning coming from the woods. Could it be that Blackjack's spirit was already plotting its revenge? Or maybe the sounds were coming from a hungry wolf pack or a lone cougar, catching the scent of freshly spilled blood? The roaring fire would keep any wildlife at bay, but just in case, Lemon hoisted his gun and kept his eyes peeled. He could defend himself against the wildlife and any desperadoes lurking about. But he wasn't so sure he could fight an avenging spirit and come out alive.

At first light, Lemon gathered his pack and readied himself to go. Rattled though he may have been, Lemon didn't forget the gold nuggets nor the placer deposits he and Blackjack had collected the day earlier. He didn't know how he'd explain his actions to the authorities, but he knew a man who might be able to help him. Father L'Heureaux would know what to do; his old friend would protect him.

Leaving Blackjack's now cold and stiffened body behind, Lemon mounted his horse and took off for the relative safety of Tobacco Plains.

Later stories said that William and Daniel Bendow had been watching the camp the entire time. The true identity of these two Native men would come into question when it was discovered that "Bendow" did not appear in the treaty list of any of the three Stoney bands living in the area. But suffice it to say the two Stoney men had allegedly seen the murder take place and had watched as Lemon paced the night away. They even had a little twisted fun of their own at Lemon's expense, taunting him with their howling noises. And they saw Lemon leave his former friend and partner carelessly heaped at the spot where he had met his fate. After ransacking what was left of the campsite, the brothers headed back to their village to report what they had seen.

The Pretended Priest

Lemon was right to assume Father Jean L'Heureaux would take him in and protect him. When he arrived in Tobacco Plains, the delirious Lemon shared his story with L'Heureaux. Any reservations the priest might have had about Lemon stumbling upon a gold mine were put to rest when Lemon showed him his poke; the gold nugget had created quite a stir to anyone who saw it, and L'Heureaux was no exception.

L'Heureaux was now faced with the problem of determining the best way to proceed. Blackjack was dead, and (in this rendition of the story) Lemon freely admitted to being the man's killer. But L'Heureaux didn't want Lemon behind bars without first discovering the location of the gold Lemon and his partner had apparently unearthed. Besides, Lemon was obviously devastated by his actions. No, it was in L'Heureaux's best interests to take Lemon in and care for his friend himself. And in the process, the priest might manage to calm the man's mind long enough to find out where he'd found the nugget gleaming up at L'Heureaux from the bottom of Lemon's weathered pouch.

To fully appreciate the kind of relationship that might have existed between L'Heureaux and Lemon, or at least to understand L'Heureaux as he exists in several accounts of the legend, a closer look at the priest is warranted. In keeping with the Wild West flavour of the lost Lemon mine story, Father Jean L'Heureaux (also spelled "LeRoux" or "Larue," depending on the source) was himself a man of questionable character, especially when it came to following the rules and expectations of his office.

Although records exist of a French Canadian at that time going by the name of Jean L'Heureaux who had once studied for the priesthood, this man never completed his education. An unnamed scandal sent him fleeing across the border into Montana. Priested or not, this man allegedly acted the role while in Montana, but his tenure only lasted until his claims of being ordained were discovered to be fraudulent. Leaving Montana, L'Heureaux again made his way into Canada and, according to Hugh Dempsey, "succeeded in convincing the Oblates at St. Albert that he was a priest." Most of his "career," however, was spent among the Blackfoot people, performing the sacraments associated with ordained ministry despite his counterfeit claims; many of his contemporaries called him the "pretended priest" to the Blackfoot.

The location where L'Heureaux lived was another detail that differed from one story to another, depending on the source of the legend. In some accounts, L'Heureaux was based in Tobacco Plains, but even that is vague. Was he at the trading post of that same name near the Montana border or at one of the Jesuit missions in BC? If the priest was based in any of these locales, the story would have taken place in what is now the East Kootenay region of BC, which would have been suicide for L'Heureaux since that part of the province was traditionally

Ktunaxa (also known as Kootenay) territory, and the Ktunaxa and Blackfoot were historically enemies. Historians suggest that as an associate of the Blackfoot, L'Heureaux would have been in danger. It seems more likely that L'Heureaux was based in Blackfoot territory in southcentral Alberta.

Several theories exist about how L'Heureaux and Lemon connected, and the nature of their relationship. But regardless which story is true, one thing appears obvious in every scenario: if Lemon did turn to L'Heureaux in his hour of need, the priest likely had other motives for helping than just fulfilling the responsibilities of his vocation.

As soon as Lemon told his story to L'Heureaux, the priest sent a Métis man named John McDougall to the scene to bury Blackjack and scout the site. The legend suggests McDougall had no trouble finding the spot where the tragedy took place; despite Lemon's allegedly muddled mind, he apparently was able to provide clear directions. McDougall reportedly interred Blackjack, whose body miraculously hadn't been devoured by wild animals, and erected a mound of stones at the site. McDougall then returned to Tobacco Plains.

L'Heureaux cared for Lemon through the winter of 1870, and the following spring, the priest urged the still-addled man to guide a team to the mountainside where Lemon said he and Blackjack had found their gold. Based on McDougall's successful attempt at locating the spot the year before, L'Heureaux had no reason to think that Lemon's current expedition would fail. But Lemon couldn't follow through with the plan. Either the man's mental state was so disturbed by the events of the previous year that he honestly couldn't remember where he and Blackjack had come to blows, or he was taken by another bout of greed and didn't want the miners to share in his find. Whatever the reason, that first return expedition came up empty-handed, and Lemon once again became crazed with emotion.

With Lemon out of commission, the priest devised another plan for finding the mine. Since McDougall didn't have any difficulty locating the mine the first time, it made sense to conclude he wouldn't have any difficulty finding it again. L'Heureaux lost no time in arranging for McDougall to lead another team.

McDougall, however, wasn't in town; he was in Fort Benton. He agreed to meet up with the new team L'Heureaux had assembled in nearby Crowsnest Lake but, sadly, he never made it to their meeting place. Having stopped over at Fort Kipp, McDougall reportedly drank rotgut whiskey, a potent mixture of wine, water, alcohol, chewing tobacco, red peppers, Jamaican ginger, black molasses and assorted other ingredients. After a night of indulging in the toxic mixture, McDougall died. Evidently, the man wasn't going to lead a party of miners anywhere, and L'Heureaux's attempt at finding Lemon's lost treasure was once again foiled.

Undeterred, the pretended priest tried again in each of the next two years, accompanying his hired guides whenever possible. The prospectors' first attempt was unsuccessful because when they reached Crowsnest Lake, they discovered a fire had decimated the forest. With no feed for the horses, the miners had no choice but to turn back.

The second attempt also ended dismally. During that expedition, L'Heureaux once again called on Lemon for help, hoping the miner had recuperated enough to lead them to the site of Blackjack's demise. Unfortunately, what little composure Lemon had regained since his experience disappeared in gradual increments the further afield the team ventured. Eventually, Lemon's growing agitation turned violent, and the group had to return to Tobacco Plains.

Lemon never again accompanied anyone on a mission to discover the now infamous mine. Thinking a change of scenery might do the man some good, L'Heureaux arranged to have Lemon travel to Texas where his brother owned a ranch. It is believed Lemon lived there until his death some years later.

Having met with one disappointment after another, L'Heureaux admitted defeat. He hung up his pickaxe for good; there were no further mentions of the priest organizing any other expeditions.

The French Connection

L'Heureaux wasn't the only would-be prospector to navigate the hillsides lining the BC and Alberta border in search of Lemon's bonanza. Lafayette French, the man who apparently bankrolled Lemon and Blackjack's original expedition, also tried to find the mine. Riley's account of French's efforts tells of how the man went about his work:

*He spent some months in the 1890s with the two survivors
of the several expeditions that had searched for the mine.*

*He even had one of them come by pack train to Crow's
Nest Lake [sic] and then north in an endeavor to have him
identify some of the landmarks in the district traveled by
the first expedition headed by Lemon. He kept La Nouse
and his band of half-breeds through the winter of 1883, in
order to check, in the spring, and discover where Lemon
and Blackjack parted company with him.*

French went so far as to contact William Bendow, one of
the two Stoney Natives purported to have witnessed Lemon
murder Blackjack. French offered Bendow "twenty five horses
and twenty five cattle" to lead him to the elusive mine. Bendow
paid a steep price for accepting the deal.

After witnessing Lemon kill Blackjack, William and his
brother Daniel returned to their village and reported what they
saw to Chief Jacob Bearspaw. Later investigations into the Bendow
brothers suggest their names may have actually been Daniel
and Paul Bigman, relatives of the chief, and that Paul may
have later had a son named King Bearspaw, a Stoney who would
in time relinquish everything he had to search for the illusive
mine in his father's story.

In any case, the chief purportedly cautioned the brothers
against telling anyone else their story. Most of all, they were
forbidden to take any white man to the site; the chief was concerned
the white man's greed over the precious metal would
bring an influx of prospectors into the area and, as a result,
destroy their hunting grounds. It was also believed that bad luck
would befall anyone returning to the site of Blackjack's murder.
For William, answering French's call to service meant going

against his own people and angering Wahcondah, the Great Spirit of the Blackfoot people.

As conflicted as William was, it has been suggested that on at least two occasions he agreed to lead French to the spot where he'd seen Lemon kill Blackjack. Both excursions were remarkably short lived. Just a day into their first outing, William was overcome with an unexplained fear, and the mission was abandoned.

On the second occasion, it seemed as though William was going to pull through after all and would lead the white men in his charge to the site so that French could finally reap the rewards of his investment. William had agreed to "camp at the old George Sage place—an abandoned ranch on the middle fork of High River—until French could get George Emerson to join them." Emerson was a Québec-born prospector who spoke both Cree and Blackfoot fluently, a valuable combination of skills given the journey ahead of them.

Once again, life had a shocking surprise in store for everyone involved when William suddenly died of an unknown cause. William's demise convinced the Blackfoot people that the spirit of Wahcondah would indeed destroy anyone foolish enough to look for the mine.

French couldn't depend on his Blackfoot friends any longer. Talk of a spirit and a curse didn't dissuade the gold digger, however. With dogged determination, and guided by a hand-drawn map that Lemon allegedly drew himself, French spent the remainder of his life trying to find Lemon's mine.

In December 1912, it appeared that French might have narrowed his search. In a letter to his friend, Senator Dan Riley, French said he'd discovered the mine and was coming to High River to give him details and enlist his help.

Perhaps the spirit of Wahcondah caught up with French after all because a few hours after posting the letter, French was severely burned when a fire consumed Emerson's cabin, where French had been staying. Journalist Thomas Primrose told of how, in an amazing attempt to survive, French crawled from the cabin near the Highwood River to the Bedingfield Ranch 3.2 kilometres away. Primrose wrote that it took the injured man several hours, and when he finally arrived at the bunkhouse, all the ranch hands were working. An exhausted French managed to hoist himself onto a bunk and sleep until help arrived. French was transported to the hospital in High River, 48 kilometres away. Although Riley visited his friend as soon as he learned of the accident, French was near death and was unable to share any details of his discovery. He died shortly thereafter.

The location of the lost mine continued to elude detection.

Going Against Tradition

The multiple, ill-fated attempts at finding the lost Lemon mine seemed to confirm in the hearts of many that the spirit of Wahcondah would curse anyone who dared unveil the legend's secrets, but one contemporary Stoney Native wasn't discouraged. Jacob Bearspaw had shared the Bendow brothers' story with his son Moses. Moses was the tribal chief, and more than likely, in time, Moses' son King would follow in his father's and grandfather's footsteps. But King had other plans. The legendary tale his father had told him over and over again throughout his youth tantalized him, and King was hungry for adventure. Moses was aware of King's preoccupation with the story so he never gave his son the mine's location.

King was so fixated by the tale that he relinquished his treaty rights in 1921, which allowed him to abandon his tribal responsibilities and scour the backcountry for the mine. King's 70-year quest to find Lemon's treasure once caused a stir near the head of the Livingstone River. A *Calgary Daily Herald* article dated February 16, 1931, with the headline "Hundreds of Prospectors Find No Trace of Gold in Livingstone Valley," explained how one of King's claims had led to a mini gold rush. The article said King had found "a piece of quartz near the summit of Flat Mountain, a peak about 5000 feet high that rises out of the east side of the Livingstone Valley."

The article went on to state that the quartz looked like a good specimen, but it hadn't been determined whether the sample contained gold or not. Even if it had, none of the prospectors working the area had found anything of value, which suggested that King's sample might have "floated" down the river from elsewhere. About a month later, a letter to the editor cast further doubt on King's claim when a Rochfort Bridge resident said he'd given King a sample of quartz he'd collected from a smelter in Trail, BC, in 1923.

King wasn't on record confirming or denying the letter-writer's suggestion. And despite King's possible deception, the dedicated prospector believed in his quest.

King never got the proof he was looking for that the lost Lemon mine was indeed a reality. He had heard the story of the mine over and over again from his mother, his grandfather and his father. As far as King was concerned, "They would not lie." King had funded his own prospecting expeditions as soon as he was old enough. "I've had it in my blood since I was a boy," King told *Nanton News* reporter Tom Primrose in July 1959. "It's been a dream to me all my life, and I guess I'd sooner look for the Lost Lemon Mine than do anything else."

Mixed Messages

There are dozens of theories about which of the lost Lemon mine stories, or which blend of stories, is nearest the truth, and what details in these various legends merit serious consideration. Riley's rendering of the story might not be the oldest written version, and several historians suggest it is riddled with errors. However, one could argue that despite the many flaws in his account, Riley personally knew several of the main characters involved, and his telling carries considerable weight.

The key characters of Lemon and Blackjack appear in many accounts about the Lemon mine, but the connection between the men isn't consistent. In most stories, Lemon discovers his bonanza with a sidekick, but it isn't always the Blackjack of Riley's account. Hugh Dempsey suggests that if the

Blackjack Riley referred to was indeed the famed Nehemia T. Smith of the Caribou Gold Rush, then he couldn't possibly fit into the story at all because 13 years after the alleged murder took place, this Blackjack was living out his last days in a Victoria hospital.

A story that appeared on October 6, 1886, in the *Calgary Daily Herald* suggests that Lemon had partnered with a crusty fellow named "Old George." In this story, the pair discovered "a good prospect somewhere on the Red Deer River in British Columbia," and shortly thereafter the pair quarrelled, which resulted in Lemon shooting Old George.

Another account suggests Lemon partnered with a man named Jim, and the two built a cabin near St. Eugene Mission, north of what is now Cranbrook, BC. In this version of the story, Jim was the unscrupulous thug, and Lemon the innocent victim who'd been shot by his partner and left for dead in their cabin while the perpetrator took off with their findings. By the time two buffalo hunters happened upon Lemon's body, he was long dead, but a note he penned before he died named Jim as his murderer and begged for justice to be done in his case.

Yet another story bestows the nickname "Blackjack" on a prospector named Jack Lemon. In this version, Blackjack is partnered with a man only known as "Dancing Bill." The pair allegedly made a strike in the Livingstone region and was crossing through high mountain passes on their way back to civilization when they were ambushed. As he tried to escape the attackers, Dancing Bill was shot dead in the back. A hunting party of Stoneys, led by a Chief Bearspaw, discovered the two men, and although they traded Lemon some moose meat and tea for some gold, the story didn't sit right with the chief. He thought it was more likely that Lemon and his partner hijacked gold from prospectors west of the Alberta border, and that Lemon killed his partner because he didn't want to split their loot. This theory echoed several other versions of the lost Lemon mine story, which suggest Lemon and Blackjack were really desperadoes themselves, making their money off the efforts of other miners.

In still another rendition of the tale, Blackjack's death was blamed on the Blackfoot who, Lemon suggested, ambushed the pair to steal their gold and supplies.

The location where these stories take place also differs depending on the source. Several of the accounts set the story in the Crowsnest Pass where, as author and geologist Ron Stewart suggests in his book, *The Lost Lemon Mine*, evidence of ancient volcanic activity could have led to the formation of "bonanza gold deposits...bonanza deposits are [an exceptionally large deposit and are] very rare but may be responsible for localized pockets of extremely rich gold ore."

Other historians place the story in the Livingstone Range, the Highwood Range, near the town of High River, near the town of Nanton, and farther south into what is now Waterton National Park. Still other sources state that since no significant gold discovery has ever occurred in Alberta, the lost Lemon mine, if it does exist, has to be located in the Kootenay region of BC.

The Real Story?

Did the prospector Lemon really exist, and if he did, who was he? Was he an honest, hard-working character who caught gold fever and murdered his partner? Or was he the victim of his partner's greed or an ambush by desperados?

If Lemon did kill Blackjack, as in Riley's version of the story, why was he never charged with the crime? And if he did murder his partner and have the wear-with-all to grab his gold as he left the scene, why didn't he follow through and return to the site? Could his actions have caused him such an extreme case of posttraumatic stress that he was never the same again?

Was it possible that Lemon was himself a desperado? And is there any truth to the suggestion that his stash of gold, the fruits of an illegal career, is hidden somewhere along Alberta's foothills? Or is the loot is hidden under the floorboards of an abandoned miner's cabin?

It also seems strange that McDougall found the mine with nothing more to go on than Lemon's half-crazed description during his first meeting with Father L'Heureaux, and that no one else came anywhere close to discovering Lemon's diggings. Surely other, experienced mountaineers would have been equally successful if the story were true?

At the same time, it doesn't make sense that so many people in the years and decades following the spring of 1870 would have spent their lives, and their life-savings, to chase a dream that had no chance of being fulfilled. Despite their discrepancies, the assorted sagas weave a tapestry that provides enough clues to suggest there must be some truth to the legend.

The hunt for answers to some of these questions prompted Alberta's most recent gold rush, which took place in the Crowsnest Pass region in 1989. At the time, Ron Stewart was taking his own soil samples in preparation for writing his book on the mine and its many legends. News reports that spring suggested Stewart had identified a 388-square-kilometre patch of land stretching throughout the Crowsnest Pass and including the town of Coleman that contained the kind of volcanic rock that could support a finding of gold. Furthermore, the samples Stewart collected seemed to confirm his theories. News reports of the day said Stewart thought there could be as much as "17 million ounces, or $7 billion worth, of gold in the area." But today, almost three decades after this discovery, exactly how much gold could potentially be unearthed, and the cost of that excavation, is still unclear.

Whether the stories behind the lost Lemon mine saga are truth or fiction, one thing is certain—the cache of gold that has been a part of Alberta's folklore for almost 150 years will continue to be spoken of for generations to come. Perhaps mining technology will evolve enough to finally pinpoint gold deposits in Alberta, or maybe a lucky vacationer will crack through the floorboards of some abandoned cabin and pull out a tattered and torn sack filled with nuggets.

Only time will tell.

MYSTERIES OF
THE DEEP

Chapter Eight

Lac Ste. Anne

~

"Tell me about the sea monster," Louis begged his great-grandmother as she tucked the five-year-old into bed for the night.

Although scared, he was nonetheless drawn by the tantalizing legend. Truth be known, sometimes he couldn't fall asleep after his great-grandmother regaled him with tales of the buffalo hunters who, tired from their hunt and making their way back to camp, found themselves in turbulent waters.

Louis wanted to hear about the legend of the Alberta lake monster that dwelled in the depths of what is now known as Lac Ste. Anne.

"Your great-grandfather saw the lake monster," Louis' great-grandmother said, describing how, after a fishing trip, her late husband had pulled his canoe onto the shoreline when a sudden wave rolled in his direction, knocking him forward. "He was lucky to have his feet on dry ground, or it would have pulled him back into the lake."

She went on to say that when her husband turned to see what prompted the sudden rough waters, he noticed his friend's canoe had capsized, and his friend was nowhere in sight. What Louis' great-grandfather did see, however, was the backside of a large creature rolling into the depths of the mysterious lake, followed by the gentle flap of its tail.

"Nobody ever saw your great-grandfather's friend again," Louis' great-grandmother said. "But it wasn't the first time the lake monster stirred the waters. It wasn't the first time the lake monster claimed one of our hunters."

"Is this for real?" the little boy asked. It was a question he asked her every time she shared the tale.

"This is what I have been told—this is the legend of your fathers." The great-grandmother patted her grandson's head and turned out the light.

~

Not much is written about the lake beast believed by some to inhabit Lac Ste. Anne; the above tale is a fictionalized version of an ancient story that is almost lost to written history. But the monster is not the only mystery surrounding the lake.

In the mid-1800s, Lac Ste. Anne was still known as "Devil's Lake" by the locals. The Cree people called the lake *Manitou Sakhahigan*, or Lake of the Spirit. The Nakota Sioux called it *Wakamne*, or God's Lake. Both traditions reference the spiritual atmosphere the people felt while at the lake. Later, when

European settlers arrived in this part of Alberta, they also recognized the celestial nature of Devil's Lake. In 1844, Roman Catholic Priest Father J.B. Thibault created the first Catholic mission built west of St. Boniface, Manitoba. The story goes that Thibault made a promise at the foot of the statue of St. Anne de Beaupre, in Québec, that "he would dedicate in her honour the first mission and church he would build in Western Canada." And so when Bishop Provencher of St. Boniface sent Father Thibault on a mission to minister to the Métis and First Nations peoples in that territory, Thibault changed the name of what many believed to be the monster-infested, turbulent waters of *Manitou Sakhahigan* to Lac Ste. Anne.

Father Thibault finished overseeing the building of the first church at the Lac Ste. Anne Mission just in time for the leaves to turn rust and gold. With the cool autumn air stirring the white-capped waters, Father Thibault held a liturgical ceremony at the renaming of the lake. The Métis, Cree and Assiniboine people who gathered at the shores of Lac Ste. Anne for the special anointing of the lake listened closely as Father Thibault prayed:

> *All ye evil spirits, I command you, in the name of the Blessed Trinity to leave the waters of this lake. Spirit of God, cover this lake with your power. Bless these waters, so that they who he instilled in the hearts of his hearers for good St. Anne, Mother of the Mother of Our Saviour, has increased with the years, thousands of Metis and Indians of many races wash themselves reverently in the waters of Lac Ste. Anne and bring home some of its water, which,*

because of their confidence in St. Anne has credited with
many cures.

–from the *Western Catholic Reporter*,
originally printed in 1961

But the initial enthusiasm surrounding the mission seemed to dwindle, and after 40-some years, the buildings at Lac Ste. Anne fell into disrepair. The church, which had been built in 1845, was in bad shape. To some it seemed as though the mission had been forgotten. And then in 1887, the priest residing over that parish was reassigned.

A Fresh Start

About that same time, the current bishop's councillor in Edmonton, Father J. Lestanc, O.M.I., was visiting Brittany, France, and said a prayer at an ancient statue of St. Anne at the Basilica of Sainte-Anne-d'Auray. But instead of feeling comfort as he prayed for direction and for those in his care, Father Lestanc felt disconnected. Why, he wondered, didn't he feel the connection he had felt in times past when he prayed to St. Anne? And then he heard what he believed was St. Anne's voice, and her rebuff was direct: "Why do you want to close down my mission?" Father Lestanc believed St. Anne was chastising him for the decisions being made about the Alberta mission, especially after the faithfulness its patron saint had shown the people of Lac Ste. Anne throughout the years. On his return to the mission, Father Lestanc spoke with Bishop Grandin about revitalizing the aging mission.

Father Lestanc's intercession worked. A new, much larger church was built in 1888. In addition, Bishop Grandin sanctioned the first pilgrimage to the shores of Lac Ste. Anne. And on June 6, 1889, 40 people travelled from the recently formed mission in St. Albert to the newly erected shrine in honour of St. Anne.

"We pray for two favours," Father Lestanc said to the people gathered on the shoreline. He prayed for rain at a time when the area was experiencing a crop-threatening drought. He also prayed that "God will give long life to St. Anne's Mission."

The rains came—and the mission of Lac Ste. Anne lives on to this day.

Since 1889, the number of people that make the annual trek continues to grow. In recent years, thousands of people, an estimated 30,000 in July 2013—members of the Catholic community, area residents and curious onlookers—walk into the waters where a monster once roamed, but which now offers them peace. They come for the experience and a blessing, and some find a healing spirit at this lake.

Since that first pilgrimage to Lac Ste. Anne's holy shores, stories of miraculous healings of all types have taken place. A pentagon-shaped structure with open sides and a peaked roof, built in 1928 after an early, similar building burned down, houses a shrine to Saint Anne. At her feet are the crutches, canes and other medical paraphernalia left behind by people who have been healed over the years. But as Father Jacques Johnson told *Alberta Sweetgrass* writer Michelle Borowiecki in 2011, many kinds of pain have been healed at this sacred place, and many kinds of blessings have been experienced. "It's not always a wooden crutch, sometimes it is a mental crutch. (They) let go of being a prisoner of anger."

As one 1961 article from the *Western Catholic Reporter* so eloquently put it, "wonderful as these temporary blessings [material healings] may be, they are in no way to be compared with the miracles performed in the souls of the pilgrims, and these are innumerable!"

No scientific studies have been conducted into the alleged cures said to have taken place at Lac Ste. Anne over the years. No detailed follow-up research has monitored the people who've professed their hearts have been uplifted, their nerves calmed, their souls revived. But it doesn't matter. For the tens of thousands of people who take part in this annual ritual, faith really is the "substance of things hoped for, the evidence of things not seen."

For the pilgrims who step onto the mission grounds and dip their feet into the cool waters, there is no mystery to the miracles that happen at that lake. They believe they are truly walking on holy ground. And that's all they need to know.

Chapter Nine

Bull Trout Mystery

~

Alberta Environment and Sustainable Resource Development says there are 65 species of fish living in Alberta's waters. Of these, 54 species are well established and are either native to the province or have been legally introduced by humans. The other 11 species can be found in limited numbers, having been brought to Alberta lakes or rivers accidentally, or illegally stocked.

The official fish of Alberta, the bull trout is one of the 54 fish species native to the province. It's found in many lakes and rivers, and on occasion will make its home in pools of fast-moving water. Bull trout also eat a lot and are known to prey on other fishes.

Herein lies the mystery, which takes us on a pilgrimage of an altogether different sort, from the prairies of north-central Alberta to the Rocky Mountains of Jasper National Park.

~

The bull trout (*Salvelinus confluentus*) is a species of char that prefers to live in cold water and at one time heavily populated Alberta's mountain-fed lakes and rivers. The body of the olive-green fish with silvery-grey sides is long and slim, especially in comparison to its large head. Along with other fish, the bull trout feeds on crustaceans and molluscs, insects floating on the water's surface and aquatic invertebrates or, as the RiverWatch Institute of Alberta puts it, the "bugs living at the bottom of a river." It's no wonder, then, that this species of fish often prefers calmer waters, rather than the turbulence found, for example, at the head of the Athabasca Falls.

The source for the huge volume of water crashing over the 23-metre drop that forms the most imposing and stunning view of the falls is the Columbia Icefield. Glacial waters from the icefield feed the Athabasca River, Jasper's largest river system, and although the Athabasca Falls isn't as high as other mountain waterfalls, the force of the glacial water pounding through the layers of quartzite and limestone have sculptured a natural wonder.

According to an information plaque located at the site, 14 species of native fish live at the base of the falls. This makes perfect sense—living at the top of the falls could prove challenging. Yet one species of fish does make its home in the turbulent headwaters. And that fish is none other than the bull trout. But how did the trout get there?

Before the flow of water over the falls produced the magnificent spectacle that draws a steady stream of tourists every day, the canyon was packed with glacial ice from the last ice age.

Once the ice melted and the water started flowing, more than 10,000 years ago, lush vegetation grew on the surrounding lands and attracted an assortment of wildlife. However, it was impossible for the bull trout to thrust itself onto the top of the falls at any point in its evolution—23 metres is a daunting leap, even for the persistent salmon that travel from the ocean to their inland spawning grounds. Besides, as one source suggests, bull trout are not typically migratory fish; they prefer a more sedentary existence.

"One theory was that during the glacial evolution of the valley, ice dams formed and fish were able to get over the falls," Jasper National Park Aquatics Specialist Ward Hughson explained. Still, if the bull trout were able to perform that feat, why weren't other species inclined to make the leap?

Hughson explained that bull trout also live at the head of other waterfalls, such as Snake Indian Falls, but they co-habit those waters with other native species. In the case of Athabasca Falls, though, the bull trout have to be pretty sharp to snap up any floating prey or bottom dwellers because there are no other species of fish for them to munch on. The limitations on their menu no doubt contribute to their much smaller size—adult bull trout in other bodies of water weigh as much as 9 kilograms whereas most bull trout at the falls weigh about 2 kilograms.

So how did this population of bull trout come to make their habitat above this tempestuous waterway? Is it possible that explorers in the late 1800s, when the bull trout was first discovered, brought the species from another location, and if so, what was the reason?

"My theory would be that a bird of prey dropped it in," Blair Yerxa of Bow River Adventures suggested. While that theory explains one possibility, the bull trout would have had to drop from the sky more than once for the fish to establish itself. When asked, Hughson admits he doesn't have the answer. "That's why it's a mystery."

Exactly how the bull trout made a home for itself at the top of Athabasca Falls is one of those mysteries that promises to baffle researchers for years to come. At this point, Parks Canada and Alberta Fisheries are focused on keeping them there; fishing for bull trout is strictly a catch-and-release option.

MURDERS, MAYHEM AND MYSTERIES OF THE HUMAN KIND

Chapter Ten

Midnight Madness: 1918 Mass Murder

~

Sleep had come quick to Dan Lough on the night of Wednesday, June 19, 1918. A lot of work would be required to transform the farm he'd just purchased from Charles Zimmer into what he envisioned for his family. It had been a long and tiring day topped off by an evening of helping his neighbours, the Snyders, put boots on their colt. The young horse was a fine specimen of an animal but a little spirited. The boots would help protect its legs during the colt's training and when it was ready to earn its keep; the fast work of herding cattle and other livestock always puts the animal at risk of injury.

Even though Lough was tired, he heard one of his children cry. Roused from his sleep, Lough swung his legs over the side of his bed and made his way down the hall. His wife Ann was sleeping soundly, and so Lough decided to check on the child himself.

"There, there," Lough murmured, brushing the hair from his child's eyes as he straightened the pillow and tucked the covers around the little one.

"Must have been a bad dream," Lough reasoned. He took one last look around the room and was about to head back to his own bed when something through the window caught his eye. Was it the light he saw flickering over at the Snyders' place, or was it a sound that caught his attention? Yes, that was it, a strange sound echoed through the otherwise peaceful night.

Lifting the windowpane in his children's room, Lough strained to make sense of the noise.

"Help! Help!"

Was that Snyder's cry he heard piercing the night air?

"Help! Help!" There it was again. Lough's heart began to race.

"I'll help you!" called a gruff, angry-sounding voice in reply.

The words didn't come from old Joseph Snyder or his nephew, Stanley. Lough was certain of it. He hadn't known his neighbours for long, but he knew them well enough to recognize the cadence of their Eastern European brogue.

Then Lough heard a deep, mournful groan that seemed to last forever before it finally softened and faded out altogether.

Struck by the urgency of the situation, Lough decided to check on his neighbours. He hastily pulled on his trousers, woke Ann to tell her where he was going and rushed outside and across the field to the Snyder farmstead.

Whatever possessed Dan Lough to make the half-kilometre dash over to the Snyder home after hearing the frightening altercation can only be attributed to adrenaline. If what he thought he heard was some kind of standoff between Snyder and some unknown assailant, charging over there might put Lough at risk of being attacked, not to mention leaving his wife and children in a rather vulnerable situation.

Lough was about 15 metres away from the building when he realized that the light he saw flickering from the vantage point of his children's bedroom was actually a fire consuming his neighbour's farmhouse. One can only imagine what Lough must have thought as he watched the flames wrap themselves around what remained of the building. Was it possible for him to rush into the burning house and rescue the two men he'd worked alongside just hours earlier? Would he make it out alive, or would he also fall victim to the conflagration? Should he run to one of the neighbouring farms and call for help, or should he run into town and get the constable?

One thought after another surged through his mind, confusing him even more. Unable to make sense of the situation, Lough decided his best bet would be to contact the police; they'd know what to do.

Rushing back to his own farm, Lough found himself waist deep into a bog. In the darkness, he had misjudged his path and bolted headlong into a slough midway between the two properties. When he finally made it back to his farmyard, Lough was in such a state that he spooked his horses. It took him a considerable amount of time to calm one down long enough to saddle it up and gallop the 3 kilometres down the road to Grande Prairie's Alberta Provincial Police (APP) offices.

Reading through the account of the events precipitating Lough's visit to the APP, it's not a stretch to understand the turmoil, the rush of emotions, the inability to fully discern the situation and the knee-jerk reactions that led him to the police rather than to another neighbour's home in search of help. Lough was still a relative newcomer to the area, which at that time was experiencing fairly rapid growth with the influx of foreign settlers looking for farming opportunities.

According to an article written by historian David Leonard, Lough and his wife had moved into a homestead outside of Sexsmith, about 20 kilometres northeast of Grande Prairie. The family had immigrated to Canada from Illinois in August 1914, so Lough was still unfamiliar with the area. He had moved into his current farmhouse in February 1918. He and the Snyders had been neighbours just a few months. It could be argued that Lough was still getting his feet wet in the neighbourhood and sought the police's help because it seemed the most logical option.

Lough arrived at the APP office around 4:00 AM. After hearing Lough's story, Corporal William Allen thought something sinister had taken place at the Snyder farm, so Allen dispatched Lough to the home of Albert Thompson. The village's liveryman owned an automobile, and by the time Lough returned for the corporal, Allen was ready to go; Lough followed on his horse.

Nothing could have prepared the men for what they saw when they arrived at the Snyder home shortly before dawn. Even with the minimal light, they could see drag marks and a blood splatter trail between a nearby log and the charred remains of the Snyders' cabin. On entering the cabin, they found the horribly burned body of a man. Investigators quickly came to the conclusion that the victim had met with foul play outside and was later pulled into the fire to destroy evidence of what must have been a murderous dispute.

As soon as Allen had arrived at the scene, he asked Thompson to return to Grande Prairie and alert Constable Hugh Jackson and the local coroner, Percy H. Belcher, that he needed their help. As the investigation continued, the body of young Stanley was discovered on the sod roof of the cabin; the sod roof was the only part of the building to survive the blaze and had caved into the building, smothering the flames and subsequently protecting what little evidence remained. An autopsy confirmed the cause of death for Stanley, as well as the burned body, which had been positively identified as Stanley's uncle. Both men were shot with a .38 calibre revolver later identified as belonging to Ignace Patan, another farmer who lived about 6 kilometres northwest of the Snyders' farm; the revolver was found at the crime site.

Based on the immediate evidence, Sergeant Patrick Egan, who headed up the Grande Prairie detachment, and Inspector Albert McDonnell, who came in to consult on the case from APP headquarters in Peace River, called the two deaths a murder-suicide. That conclusion would later come into question when another investigator pointed out that the revolver had been discovered on the sod roof. Stanley had been shot behind his left ear. Joseph had been shot under one eye, making him the more likely suicide victim. But it wouldn't have been possible for Joseph to toss the revolver onto the sod roof, where it now lay, after killing himself. And what about the drag marks leading up to the cabin, and the blood stains trailing from the log to where the front door once was? A murder-suicide scenario didn't explain those clues, nor did it answer the question about why Patan's gun was found at the scene.

Unfortunately, this first theory diminished any sense of urgency the authorities might initially have had, along with any chance at setting up a proper patrol of the area and apprehending a suspect. Residents of the village of Grande Prairie and its surrounding district were convinced the police had made a hasty decision.

A Second Crime Scene

Any lingering doubt that a murder-suicide had occurred at the Snyder farm was almost completely erased three days later when Alex Peebles visited the APP. One account explains that the farmer said he'd noticed some of Patan's horses in his grain field. Thinking that Patan wasn't aware his horses had wandered, Peebles decided to have a word with his neighbour after chasing the horses out and repairing the fence.

As Peebles approached the Patan shack, he noticed right away that something seemed off. The wagons Patan had loaded for a trip north he and two other men were taking were still there, and yet the trio was supposed to have left days ago.

Sources differ as to what happened next. Newspaper reports of the day state that Peebles was "horrified to find the dead bodies of three men. Two in the house and one in the wagon covered over with canvas." Dr. Leonard's article on the murders suggested Peebles tried the door, but it was locked, and Peebles was discouraged from exploring further by "a vicious dog" on the premises.

Perhaps Peebles peered through a window when he tried to open the door, which would explain the newspaper story's suggestion that he'd seen the bodies. Either way, since Inspector McDonnell was still in town, he took charge of the complaint and sent Sergeant Egan and a Corporal S. McPherson to check on things.

If they thought the scene at the Snyder farm was disturbing, it was nothing compared to what greeted them at the Patan place.

The door had to be forced open before Egan and McPherson could enter the home. The smell must have bowled them over: inside the house were the ripe and decomposing bodies of Patan and his friend, James Wudwand. Patan was a Polish-born farmer who'd immigrated from Illinois a while earlier, and Wudwand was a Russian-born livery stable worker. Both were covered with "canvas and bedding," which no doubt would not have prevented bugs from feasting on their corpses.

A 2011 *Calgary Herald* story penned by reporter Jana Pruden tells of how German trapper Charles Zimmer was found in a wagon on the property, "his head visible under the sacks of flour and sugar that had been piled on top of his body, recognizable to the men who found him by his dark, bushy beard and the bright gold tooth shining at the front of his dentures." Pruden goes on to describe how the fourth and final murder victim, Frank Parzychowski, a Ukrainian blacksmith hailing from North Dakota, was discovered lying on his back with "one hand in his overall pocket, the other raised over his head as if he'd been trying to protect himself."

Patan's throat was slashed; the rest of the men had been shot. Like the gun found at the Snyders, a .38 calibre revolver was the weapon used in the murders. Judging by the state of decomposition of the four bodies, the .38 calibre revolver found at the Snyder place and the five spent shell casings in the gun, it was reasonable to assume the same perpetrator was responsible for all six murdered men. Police believed that although they were dealing with two crime scenes, the murders were connected. They were looking for one murderer, or perhaps a murderer and an accomplice. And judging by the accuracy of the aim, the murderer was one hell of a good shot.

According to the *Grande Prairie Herald* of Tuesday, July 2, 1918, Percy H. Belcher headed the coroner's inquest. The case was heard on Wednesday, June 26, just a week after the first two murders had taken place. It had originally been scheduled for June 25, but with the subsequent discovery at the Patan house, the case was pushed back one day so all six murders could be examined at the same time. Ten witnesses took the stand, includ-ing Dr. Conroy and Dr. M.L. MacDonald of Lake Saskatoon who performed the post mortems in the Snyder shootings.

Most of the witnesses spoke solely to the character of the victims. Witnesses stated that it was common knowledge that three of the four men gathered at the Patan house would have had large quantities of cash on their person having "recently sold their winter's catch of furs." Zimmer also had the $2000 he made from selling his farm to Dan Lough, and together it was estimated the trio had $5000 in cash.

Dan Lough was the only person who'd come forth with anything close to first-hand information in the Snyder case.

What was Lough doing at the Snyder farm the night before the murders, Crown Prosecutor E.B. Cogswell asked.

"Helping the elder man place boots on a young colt," replied Lough.

"Was anyone else present?" Cogswell continued.

"The younger man had been around the premises..."

Cogswell asked Lough if he thought the two Snyders got along.

"Both appeared to be on the usual friendly terms."

Cogswell then asked Lough if he and the elder Snyder had noticed anything unusual while they were working on the colt—anything at all that might have taken their attention off their task.

Lough explained that while he and Snyder were "working on the colt in the stable, the horses feeding on the other side of a slough lying to the south of the shack came rushing across the slough and up through the yard." Lough went on to explain how he and both Snyder men "walked down to the slough to see what had caused the stampede, but saw nothing."

Lough went on to retell the events that led up to him hearing calls for help at the Snyder farm.

"That was it," Lough said. There was nothing more he could tell them.

Lough's testimony was enough for the jury at the inquest to render a verdict of "willful murder in both cases."

It was official—the Alberta Provincial Police had a mass murder on their hands, and they were grasping at straws to hone in on a suspect.

If Lough thought he was finished with the Snyder business after testifying at the coroner's inquest, he was sadly mistaken.

Lough may have thought he'd done his best to be a good neighbour by putting himself at risk for his fellow man and doing his civic duty by alerting the authorities of the fire before finally retelling everything he knew of the night in question. But before the sad story of Alberta's largest mass murder to date would be put to rest, Lough would find himself behind bars and fighting to protect his own life and restore his good name.

Under a Magnifying Glass

With six murders on their hands, and a considerable amount of time having lapsed after the murders were committed, investigators knew they needed to work fast if they ever hoped to solve this mystery. Police interviews with residents revealed that money could have been a motive for the murders. They learned that Patan, Wudwand and Zimmer had withdrawn large sums of money from the Union Bank in Grande Prairie on June 18—sources speculate that collectively they pulled $3700. The three men were planning a 530-kilometre trek to Fort Vermilion to buy a ranch. It looked as though it was simply bad luck that Parzychowski was at the scene at all; he had stopped by that evening to have a drink with his buddies before they left and was probably killed as collateral damage.

But how did the Snyders fit into this scenario? Peebles told police he saw five people in Patan's farmyard around 10 o'clock on the night of the murders, but he wasn't close enough to positively identify them. Was it possible Snyder was there too and was also killed because he could identify the murderer?

While police were examining the sadly compromised murder scenes that had not been secured from the public, a pair of suspects in a string of robberies gave Corporal Allen and Constables Bremner and McMullen a run for their money. The two simultaneous major cases were stretching the already thin supply of police members to its limits. But investigators were anxious to capture the two robbers who'd been seen leaving

Grande Prairie in the early morning hours of June 20. The police wanted to rule out any connection the pair of desperadoes might have to the mass murder case.

Earl "Shorty" Salisbury was captured after crossing the Wapiti River south of Grande Prairie on Wednesday, June 26. The police and their trapper guides, Sam Raymond and Tommy Foote, apprehended Salisbury at "a cache where he and his party had assembled quite a stock of provisions." Salisbury surrendered without incident. He explained that he and Norman Keeler were looking for land to homestead, and at that moment Keeler was building a shack in the bush.

With Salisbury leading the way, the posse located Keeler without any difficulty. Both men were charged with theft and found guilty during a preliminary trial held on June 29. They were sentenced to six months behind bars.

The circumstances surrounding the arrest cast suspicion on Keeler and Salisbury, and residents of Grande Prairie and its surrounding farming community must have wondered if the pair was also responsible for the six murders, but the two men denied any knowledge of the tragedy. And although they had stolen property, they weren't in possession of the money said to have been carried by three of the men at the Patan farm. As the *Herald* noted, there was "little or no evidence to show that they were in any way connected with the murders." The authorities agreed, and no charges were laid on the two robbers in relation to that case.

The police continued to work diligently on the two murder scenes, but they noticed a growing tension among area residents. Investigators were finding that they, too, were being examined under a public magnifying glass. And as the days and weeks wore on with no suspect identified or charged, anxiety turned to anger for both the police and the public.

Grande Prairie was still a village when the 1918 mass murder occurred, and less than a decade old, but it was a budding metropolis when compared to the otherwise rustic parts of the province. The addition of a railway in 1916 had attracted new settlers to the region, which required an increase in essential services, and the police had to patrol the more than 6000 people living in the district. Limited funds and a lack of "suitable men" because of World War I made policing more difficult. A front-page editorial in the July 16 edition of the *Grande Prairie Herald* spelled out the situation in detail:

> *We have felt for a long time that the Alberta Police Force was inadequate but we certainly did not realize the extent of their inadequacy until the recent killings showed them up.*

> *In the first place the district is entirely too large to be handled by the number of men in charge. The R.N.W.M.P. never had less than 6 men in the territory where the present Provincial system has only 2, with at least 2000 more settlers.... The men on detachment are as a rule efficient enough, although the best men on the force have been driven out by the apparent ignorance of the men higher up....*

Although the editorial tactfully supported the officers, it also went on to point out that the Snyder murders were discovered within two hours of their occurrence, and had police adequately patrolled the crime scene and the surrounding area, they may have been able to "apprehend all those who could not give a satisfactory account of themselves" and, therefore, have better success in pinpointing a suspect. The large gap between the discovery of the crime and the onset of an official investigation would have given even the most careless of criminals enough time to devise an alibi.

The editorial also questioned the murder at the Patan farm. Why had the police not investigated the Patan home as soon as they learned the revolver found at the Snyders' belonged to Patan? Instead, another civilian, Peebles, had to inform police of the second crime.

Perhaps the public pressure was wearing on the authorities, but by the end of July, Chief Detective J.D. Nicholson arrived in Grande Prairie. Despite the contamination of both crime scenes by curious onlookers, Nicholson conducted his own investigation and also interviewed residents again. Although the passage of time can often dim recollections, it can also have the reverse effect, he reasoned, and Nicholson was hoping to unearth new memories and catch a new lead.

By the middle of August, Nicholson had provided the Deputy Attorney General with the names of five men that Nicholson thought were persons of interest in the case. These men were considered suspects because they were acquainted with all six victims, they each knew of the victims' plans to travel to Fort Vermilion, and they were all aware of that Patan and Zimmer were carrying large amounts of cash.

Leading Nicholson's list of suspects at that time was none other than Dan Lough.

Under Suspicion

Lough had a few additional strikes going against him when compared with the other suspects. He had been with Joseph Snyder on the night he was murdered, and there was only his word that he'd left the man alive some time around 10 that night. Lough was also the person who later found the first two bodies. Furthermore, the only set of tracks discovered at the Snyder farm were said to belong to Lough.

Lough said he was wet up to his waist when he went to the police because he'd stumbled into a bog when rushing back to his farm. Nicholson believed Lough could have fabricated this excuse to cover up the real reason why he was wet—he had washed the victims' blood off his clothes. In addition, Nicholson thought it highly suspicious that when he visited Lough one morning, hoping to ask him a few more questions, the family's door wasn't locked. Nicholson suggested this was odd given that other residents in the district were so spooked that they made sure to bolt their doors. Lough wasn't frightened because he was the murderer, Nicholson reasoned. He also thought it was strange that Lough went to the police instead of going to a neighbour for help.

Nicholson further theorized that Lough may have told Snyder that he was planning to visit the Patan farm that fateful

June night. After Lough committed the four murders, presumably to rob the men of their cash, he had no choice but to kill the Snyders as well to keep them from talking to the police.

Nicholson's arguments were thin on several points. For one thing, if Lough did rob the men of their money, why wasn't the money ever found? If Lough killed the Snyders to keep them from talking, why was he in such a hurry to report the crime to the police? Wouldn't it have served him better to lay low until the police discovered the bodies on their own and spoke with him during their subsequent investigation? With both the Snyder men dead, he didn't have to admit to visiting them at all.

To say Nicholson's reasoning was flawed is an understatement. But after two more years of investigation, and no further suspects, Nicholson felt pressure, both from residents and his superiors, to make an arrest. Despite the report he filed with Deputy Attorney General A.G. Browning advocating for Lough's arrest, Nicholson later admitted he didn't have sufficient evidence to make his case and arrested Lough for the Snyders' murders on June 20, 1920. Regardless, the courts moved forward with the charges. Two days later when Magistrate Percy Belcher heard the case, Lough pleaded not guilty in a calm clear voice. He was incarcerated until his trial on December 9 and 10.

In his argument against the prosecution, Defence Attorney Martin Eagar argued there was no evidence to support the claim that Lough was ever at the Patan residence on the night of the murders. Most rational citizens would have rushed to the police if they were Lough, not to a neighbour, as Nicholson suggested. Furthermore, Lough's wife Ann had backed her husband's story; unfortunately, Ann and the couple's youngest child had succumbed to the Spanish flu epidemic in 1918 so her testimony couldn't be verified.

Lough's lawyer addressed point after point, damaging Nicholson's already flimsy case for any reasonable juror. There was simply no evidence to support the charges facing his client, Eagar surmised. Trusting the jury to make the correct call, the defence rested.

It took the jury less than an hour to bring in its verdict.

"Not guilty!"

Lough was no doubt eager to celebrate his release from custody with his three children, who'd been placed in an Edmonton children's shelter during his incarceration, but he remained stoic to the end.

Some might argue that the only reason he was arrested was so investigators could save face after what many suggested had been a botched investigation. Not long after the trial, Lough took his children back to Illinois.

Other Suspects

Lough wasn't the only suspect Nicholson had examined during his two-year search. Frank Lakosky was a local veteran who, one might argue from today's perspective, may have suffered from posttraumatic stress, though the talk of the day was that Lakosky was a manic-depressive, or just plain crazy. It was also common knowledge that Lakosky was a sharp shooter, and that he'd killed his fair share of German soldiers during the war. Perhaps he'd lost his mind and, in a fit of rage, committed the murders. But there was never any concrete evidence to proceed with charges against him.

Richard Knight was another suspect. He was a rogue Sexsmith-area bootlegger who had bragged about making some "easy money." But Knight had a solid alibi; several witnesses reported seeing him in Sexsmith when the murders occurred.

Dr. David Leonard also pointed to F.R. Beckham, agent at Grande Prairie's Western Trust, as another candidate for the crime. Beckham had taken "over the assets of the murdered men and also seemed wealthier than his salary would allow." Detective Sullivan reportedly called Beckham the "master criminal in the murders" who "slept with a revolver" and called out "murder" in his sleep. Again, no solid evidence was ever discovered against the man, so no charges were laid.

And then there was a rather inconspicuous article that appeared in the *Herald* on July 18, 1918:

$400 Found in Victim's Shack

The finding of $400.00 in cash by one of the murdered men's wives some number of days after the recent murders were committed and after the premises were thoroughly searched by the police a number of times, leads one to wonder at the apparent lack of efficiency in the methods employed in the investigation of the recent murders. Perhaps the rewards offered at the present time will cause a greater and more exhaustive search of the evidence at hand.

The official deposition of Frank Parzychowski's widow told a slightly different version of the find at the Patan residence. Rosie Parzychowski explained that a "friend" had a premonition that "about" $450 in gold was hidden somewhere at the site. Rosie knew her husband had some gold, but nothing was recovered during the police investigation. Following the premonition, Rosie asked the police for permission to search the place. Amazingly, she did recover $440 in gold in an "old boot in the woodshed." Since Rosie was away in Washington State at the time of the murders, she wasn't a suspect in the crimes.

Richard Knechtel, however, was another story.

Knechtel and Rosie married just six months after Frank was murdered. Knechtel and Patan were also at odds with one another at the time of the murder, and Knechtel reportedly told a neighbour that he would "fix [Patan] one day."

Nicholson eventually charged Knechtel with the murder, but the charges were dropped when Magistrate Belcher dismissed the case, citing a lack of any "incriminating evidence."

Conclusion

The *Grande Prairie Herald* correctly predicted the outcome of the mass murder investigation just weeks after the murders were discovered:

> *Much valuable time has been lost; and it is doubtful when, if ever, these murderers will ever be apprehended. Some of the men in charge of the case are capable and experienced,*

but lacking in the necessary support and are late on the ground. What is going to be done to remedy these conditions we do not know, but something should be done immediately, if our wives and families are not to be terror stricken any longer.

Although the 1918 case remained open for many years, no one was ever charged with the murders, and for those who knew of the tale it became a gripping mystery that demanded an answer. Throughout the 1990s, Albertan Wallace Tansem breathed new life into the old, moth-beaten case. The amateur historian spent the last 10 years of his life researching old files, inquest reports and newspaper articles in an effort to solve the murders. In an extreme effort to find out the truth, Tansem travelled to Illinois to interview Lough's descendants, and he also wrote a book on the story. Unfortunately, his manuscript wasn't completed before his death in 2001. A decade later, in 2010, the story was revisited once again when Dr. David Leonard authored his article for *Alberta History*.

Despite all the interest the case generated, both when it occurred and over the years, it remains unsolved, leaving us all to wonder how someone could murder six people in two different locations in an area with a relatively small population and not leave behind a single solid clue to his identity.

Chapter Eleven

The Murder of MaryAnn Plett

~

MaryAnn Plett shook her head as she turned the television off for the night. According to the recent news reports, there were no new leads in the disappearance of Mr. and Mrs. Clint Armstrong who had left their home in Holden, Alberta, to visit their daughter in Peace River. It was a trip that should have been restful and joyful. Instead, a daughter and her family, overwhelmed with worry, were desperate for answers.

Ten days had passed—that couldn't be good news. The couple obviously wasn't just late or having car trouble somewhere. Holden is an hour from Edmonton, and a six-hour drive from Peace River. The Armstrongs should have made that trek in a day, no problem. Something tragic must have happened to them, MaryAnn and her husband Jake agreed as they turned the lights off and headed to bed that crisp September evening in 1971.

The Armstrongs had disappeared into thin air—car and all. How do two people and their car just vanish like that? Jake would be asking himself that same question yet again the next evening—only the subject in question wouldn't be the Armstrongs; it would be his very own wife.

~

The morning of September 15, 1971, started out much like any other school day. With two boys to dress and feed, lunches to make and her own busy work agenda to iron out, 29-year-old MaryAnn Plett attacked the day with her usual enthusiasm and vigour.

This behaviour was typical for MaryAnn, who was as efficient and organized in her career as a real estate agent as she was a dedicated and loving housewife and mother. She thrived on being busy and took great pride in providing for her young family while her husband completed his university education.

But MaryAnn was anything but typical. In 1971, married women most often worked in the home. And although the Women's Liberation Movement of the 1960s pried open the doors for women to enter what were at that time male-dominated occupations, this philosophy was never the motivation for MaryAnn's venture into real estate. She simply started selling houses because she felt a "calling" to do so. A devote and charismatic Christian, MaryAnn believed God was directing her to peruse the want ads back in May 1968, shortly after the family moved into their new home in Edmonton. Days later she was working in the north-end office of Edmonton's Graham Realty.

The Criminal Mind of a Stalker

MaryAnn was one of the province's first female real estate agents, and it was a career that had won her a great many accolades. She got personal satisfaction from knowing that she'd made a difference in the lives of the people she met. With her help, families found the home of their dreams on a budget they could afford or sold their properties when life circumstances dictated that need.

The latter situation was MaryAnn's focus that autumn morning in 1971. Clients of hers desperately wanted to sell their Looma acreage. MaryAnn had just sold Grant and Joyce Nelson a new home in Edmonton, and the financial strains of two mortgages, coupled with health concerns, left the couple financially and emotionally drained. MaryAnn felt empathy for the Nelsons and believed they would gain peace of mind if only she could sell the Looma acreage, she told Jake during their morning prayers. After kissing Jake goodbye and seeing seven-year-old Nelson and five-year-old Lyndon off to school, MaryAnn headed to her office with renewed resolve. Maybe this day would bring her closer to helping her clients sell their property. And maybe, just maybe, she'd get another call from that mysterious Mr. Cooper.

Odd as the man was, MaryAnn welcomed another chance to talk with James Cooper. She'd had a few occasions to speak with the stocky, middle-aged man who had a "gruff voice" and a tendency to argue under his breath. The strange gent presented himself as a businessman from Winnipeg who worked with a large American-based, "mud-pump company in the oil industry."

Sun reporter Pamela Roth, who revisited the unsolved murder in a 2012 article, explained that Cooper told MaryAnn he needed a "property with a clearing to store heavy equipment, but wanted the view of the clearing blocked from the road for privacy." MaryAnn believed the Looma property was a perfect fit. As uneasy as the man made her feel, MaryAnn hoped she'd have another chance to try to sell the idea to him.

As luck would have it, MaryAnn didn't have to wait long to have her wish met. When she arrived at work that Wednesday morning, MaryAnn learned that Cooper had called for her again. The secretary at Graham Realty said Cooper had asked to set up an appointment to see the property one more time. This would be the man's third visit; MaryAnn had toured him through the acreage on August 23 and September 9. Maybe three times was a charm? Maybe this time he'd pull out his chequebook and make an offer? MaryAnn definitely hoped this was the case. She was well equipped to deal with most clients, and God knew how she turned over some of her more difficult ones to Him in prayer, but she really didn't know how long she'd be able to put up with Cooper and his odd behaviour.

In fact, Cooper was so peculiar that the usually easy-going MaryAnn told her co-workers and her husband that she didn't feel safe driving alone with him to the acreage. The man refused to give MaryAnn any of his contact information, and he never met MaryAnn at her office. Instead, MaryAnn was always instructed to meet Cooper at the parking lot of the Bonnie Doon

Shopping Centre. At each meeting Cooper would suddenly knock on the window of MaryAnn's two-tone green Pontiac and slip into the passenger's seat. He was always late and never apologized for keeping MaryAnn waiting. She never noticed Cooper coming out of or returning to a vehicle; he just seemed to materialize. This strange fact would later lead investigators to believe the man may have lived near the southside shopping centre and not in Winnipeg as he claimed to MaryAnn.

MaryAnn must have coached herself before driving Cooper the 30 kilometres from Bonnie Doon to Looma just one more time. A lot of potential buyers need a third visit before committing to a deal. But after that, she might have to call his bluff and refuse any further requests to see the property.

Perhaps Cooper sensed MaryAnn was becoming disillusioned with his professed interest; unfortunately, MaryAnn never had that opportunity to decline another request.

A Rocky Night

Jake was feeling unsettled long before he received the telephone call from Norm Schultz late in the afternoon of September 15. Jake had only one class that morning, so he'd spent the majority of the day at home with his son Lyndon and had made at least one unsuccessful attempt to call his wife at her office. The secretary had told Jake that MaryAnn was showing the Looma property to Cooper again; a fact that left Jake with a knot in the pit of his stomach. The subsequent call from Schultz, his wife's manager, tightened that knot considerably.

Schultz asked Jake if he'd heard from MaryAnn. Since she'd left with Cooper to Looma earlier that day, no one in the office had heard from her. That was unusual behaviour for Mary-Ann. She was always careful to update the office as to her whereabouts throughout the workday, especially when it came to dealing with clients like Cooper. No phone calls and no Mary-Ann by that point in the day had left her co-workers concerned.

Neither Jake nor Schultz lost any time springing into action. After hiring a babysitter, Jake met Schultz at MaryAnn's office, and the two men raced to Looma. When they arrived and didn't see MaryAnn's car anywhere on site, the two men split up. Jake started knocking on doors, asking if anyone had seen his wife or the couple's car, and Schultz called the office. Before long, MaryAnn's co-workers, accompanied by representatives from the Sherwood Park Fire Department, converged on the site and started a ground search. By then the sun was fading fast, so searchlights were necessary to scour the area as best as they could while searchers called MaryAnn's name over a loud-speaker. But nothing was uncovered—not a single clue to suggest MaryAnn was ever there that day.

After driving along each of the several routes between the Looma property and Edmonton, and questioning workers at every gas station they passed in the hope that someone would have noticed the young woman buying gas or a coffee for the road, the group reconvened back at the Graham Realty's south-side office, which at that time was located on Whyte Avenue and 107 Street. It was nearing midnight when someone finally called Edmonton police about the missing woman. Not sure where to turn at that moment, and cognizant of the two little boys he'd left in someone else's care, Jake decided to return home. Just as he was opening the office door to leave, he noticed what he believed was a strange man driving his wife's car along Whyte Avenue in front of the office. Jake and some of MaryAnn's co-workers jumped into a car, hoping to chase the Pontiac down and question the driver, but by the time they were on the road, the Pontiac was nowhere to be seen.

A dejected Jake must have felt like he was in a very bad dream.

It was a nightmare that wasn't about to end anytime soon.

One Long Night Continues

Jake had been away all evening. By the time the tired father returned home, the babysitter had put the Plett's boys to bed for the night; it was the first of many out-of-the ordinary experiences the young children would experience over the next year.

Shortly after Jake arrived back home, the police showed up. They wanted to issue a missing person's bulletin, but Jake was reticent about what information should be included. He wanted to contact their extended family about MaryAnn's disappearance before too many details were released to the public, and so only the description of the car and its licence plate number went out at that point.

In addition to gathering as much information on Mary-Ann's disappearance as possible, the police were anxious to have a look at the Looma property for themselves. And so Jake left his home again; for a second time that night the boys were left in the care of a babysitter while a search party reconvened at the acreage. Things can look very different in the darkness of night. It was about 3:00 AM, wet and windy, when Jake, Gail Cote, one of MaryAnn's co-workers, and the police arrived at the property. Jake was convinced he saw fresh tire tracks on the driveway, but the rain made it impossible to tell for sure.

By the time Jake returned home, his boys were up and asking after their mother. Convening a family meeting, Jake explained to all of his loved ones that MaryAnn was missing. And while everyone was clinging to the hope that she would be found alive and well, the unvoiced fear that she'd been abducted, perhaps even murdered, was beginning to impose itself into everyone's thoughts.

In his book, *Valley of Shadows*, Jake wrote how that day in September changed his life and "nearly shattered" him. "It was the day in which we stepped into the Valley of Shadows, where the darkness was almost overwhelming."

Examining the Evidence

Statistically speaking, most murders are committed by someone known to the victim. According to 2011 statistics, homicides committed by a stranger or unknown assailant accounted for only 15.6 percent of cases, a statistic that is fairly representative of homicides.

Although a body had not been discovered, it's no surprise that Jake found himself on the receiving end of an interrogation with respect to his wife's disappearance. "The spouse is generally considered the prime suspect unless proven otherwise," retired Edmonton police inspector Joe Poss told *Edmonton Journal* reporter Wilfred Golbeck in a 1992 article about the Plett case.

Although the suspicions devastated Jake, he faced his interrogators without reservation and even volunteered to undergo a polygraph test, which he passed with flying colours. Satisfying investigators, Jake was removed from the list of suspects. In reality, the list was a short one. Cooper was now the investigators' main suspect. Unfortunately, no one from MaryAnn's office had ever seen or spoken with the man.

While the search for MaryAnn continued, the hunt for Mr. Cooper was also underway. Police hoped to uncover some more concrete evidence when the Pletts' Pontiac mysteriously appeared in the used car section of Don Wheaton's car sales lot two days after MaryAnn's disappearance. But the abandoned car added more mystery than clues in the case. With few exceptions, the car had been meticulously cleaned. Aside from a wig, which Jake confirmed had belonged to his wife, and a pair of sunglasses that Jake denied belonged to either of them, the car was empty. Where were the clip-on sunglasses that Jake and his wife kept in the car? Where were the car registration and warranty papers the couple usually kept in a plastic binder? Whatever happened to MaryAnn's briefcase, along with other personal items Jake knew were usually kept in the family's vehicle?

Worse still, investigators discovered smudges of blood on the trunk latch and the rug in the trunk. Although the individual responsible for this mystery was thorough in his cleaning efforts, he'd left enough evidence behind to confirm one thing for investigators: the blood in the car was indeed MaryAnn's. The blood all but confirmed investigators' worst fears; MaryAnn's case had evolved from a disappearance to a probable homicide.

A veritable army of law enforcement worked on Mary-Ann's disappearance. Sixteen constables and 33 Canadian Forces personnel from Namao, Alberta, assisted Leduc RCMP, whose jurisdiction included the Looma property, in an organized shoulder-to-shoulder search of the property. Police dogs also joined in the hunt, which included the drainage of a slough on the property.

To the north, Edmonton investigators combed city streets and back lanes for the missing woman and searched hotels and motels for the illusive James Cooper. Family and friends of the Pletts were also getting involved in the search efforts; they wrote, printed and delivered flyers asking for information about the missing woman. And on October 11, almost a month after MaryAnn disappeared, more than 200 family, friends and concerned citizens joined the Leduc RCMP for yet another search of a 32-kilometre radius surrounding the Looma property in a last-ditch hope of unearthing something concrete before the winter covered the prairies with its typical thick blanket of snow.

The concerted efforts of everyone involved seemingly covered as many bases as anyone could think of. Sadly, the hard work didn't produce a single clue. Worse, MaryAnn was still missing, and her husband and sons were in mourning.

Spreading the Word

Although hard clues weren't forthcoming, the publicity garnered by all the search efforts achieved one major result—it kept MaryAnn's case in the public spotlight. It was perhaps because her disappearance was so well known that on October 30, James Boyd and Max Leingrand had the wherewithal to call Swan Hills RCMP after they discovered a briefcase while bird hunting about 29 kilometres southwest of Fort Assiniboine. In his book, Jake explained that, "the briefcase had been found behind three pines about 50 feet from the road." It looked like it may have been tossed there from the road, Jake mused.

The briefcase indeed belonged to MaryAnn. According to the 1992 *Edmonton Journal* article, a search of the area over the next day or so would uncover more items that belonged to the missing Edmonton woman: "a can opener, curler and some papers." Unfortunately, winter in Alberta often means heavy snowfall. That investigators were able to uncover the selection of items so late into the fall was something of a miracle. But their luck didn't hold up for long. Two days later, Mother Nature dumped 10 centimetres of snow, a veritable blanket covering everything in sight. Although Jake knew of the discovery, he was sworn to secrecy—he couldn't even share the news with the rest of the family. The weather imposed a hiatus on any kind of formal search, leaving the area vulnerable to public curiosity, and investigators didn't want locals probing about and potentially destroying evidence in the process.

Investigators renewed their search in the spring after employees from the Pinto Creek Sawmill reported yet another strange discovery on Friday, April 14, 1972. Women's clothing had been discovered near a drainage ditch. A subsequent search of the region unearthed a part of a woman's skull, a fragment of a femur and other small bones left behind after scavengers and rodents had worked over the deceased woman's body. A visual identification was impossible, but Dr. John Woytuck, the Pletts' dentist, positively identified the few dental remains collected as those belonging to MaryAnn Plett.

It was official. Jake now had a funeral to plan, and investigators were more focused than ever on finding the murderer.

More than 900 people attended MaryAnn's service. Jake was no longer a person of interest in his wife's disappearance, but the strange Mr. Cooper was still number one on the list of potential suspects. Was it possible that Cooper might want to revisit his crime and would turn up at the funeral? Police took photos of as many of the 900 mourners as possible, but after consultation with the family, they were unable to identify anyone who might fit the description MaryAnn had given of the man to her co-workers.

When thrust into the middle of a tragedy like the one the Plett family had to endure, it's hard to imagine life could regain any semblance of normalcy. But despite the fact that Jake would spend the rest of his life keeping his deceased wife's memory alive, and praying for a resolution, he did have a modicum of healing. Jake eventually married a woman named Marion, and the couple had a baby girl named Carlene. Unfortunately, Jake and his new wife died in a plane crash in 1978, just nine days before their daughter's fourth birthday.

Although the case remains open, and investigators no doubt have some clues that haven't been released to the public, the mysterious disappearance and murder of MaryAnn Plett is as far from being solved as it was when it took place more than 40 years ago.

Many questions remained unanswered about the case. Some investigators have suggested that MaryAnn Plett appeared to be an intentional victim, but why? Was sexual assault the motive? Or was she targeted because she was a woman succeeding in what was then a male-dominated career?

Who was Mr. James Cooper? Was he really a businessman from Winnipeg, or was he a spurned admirer that lived in Edmonton? Did he indeed have a car, or did he live in the Bonnie Doon area and walk to meet MaryAnn?

If Cooper was indeed guilty of this horrendous crime and had set his sights on MaryAnn, why was he so fixated on her? Had he been watching her for a prolonged period of time, or was she a random victim he came across one day and arbitrarily chose as his target? And if she was a random victim, had others met the same fate by his hands?

Did Cooper drive her directly to the place where what was left of her body was eventually discovered, or did he kill her elsewhere as one investigator suggested? And if that was the case, was the murderer more mobile than at first thought? Did he know the Fort Assiniboine area, as another investigator suggested, or was it a random dumpsite?

Why did the murderer allegedly drive past Graham Realty's Whyte Avenue office the night of MaryAnn's disappearance? And why did he abandon her car at the Don Wheaton dealership? Was he trying to taunt the authorities with the belief that he had gotten away with the perfect crime, or did he have some hidden motive for his actions?

MaryAnn Plett's abduction and murder has so captivated Albertans that every few years another article appears in one of the Edmonton dailies, revisiting the case in the hope that someone with that vital clue needed to solve the case might come forward. MaryAnn's son Nelson has been interviewed on occasion. He said both he and his brother, Lyndon, haven't given up hope that at some point the questions surrounding their mother's untimely demise might be answered.

Nelson also said that if and when that time comes, they hope they can find it in their hearts to forgive the perpetrator. "My dad always said that if and when this guy was ever caught that he would go and tell him that he forgives him," Nelson told *Sun* reporter Pamela Roth in 2012. "My brother and I both said as difficult as it might be, if it was ever solved, we would try and honour Dad's wishes."

Chapter Twelve

Gone But Not Forgotten: A Call for Justice

~

Twenty-five-year-old Jennifer pulled her sweater tight against her body as she power-walked the two blocks to her home from her part-time job at a nightclub on Whyte Avenue. Despite the late hour and enveloping darkness, the close proximity between the two places made using her car, or even taking a bus, a ridiculous waste of money for the university student. Besides, Jennifer reasoned, she enjoyed the fresh air and a walk after a shift of serving drinks in a smoky bar.

Still, these late-night walks were leaving an increasingly unsettled feeling in the pit of her stomach. Edmonton had experienced unseasonably warm temperatures that February, but a cold pall had settled on the city that had little to do with the cooler, much greyer, month of March. Just thinking about the last seven weeks sent chills through Jennifer's body. Two women had disappeared within a week of each other, the body of one of the women was discovered the next day, removing any doubt that there was a dangerous predator lurking. And then there was the unsolved murder of a 19-year-old woman the previous September.

People were starting to worry that a serial killer was on the loose, and Jennifer's mother had repeatedly asked her daughter to take a taxi home when she worked late.

Maybe she should start taking a cab home, Jennifer thought as she punched in the security code to her building and let herself inside. She was home safe and sound for that night, but perhaps she was tempting fate. Maybe, until the police finally arrested someone and solved these cases, she should start using some of her tip money to ensure her safety. Her mother's fears would certainly be assuaged, and if Jennifer was honest with herself, she'd feel a lot less anxious, too.

If all the young women of Edmonton had decided to stick close to home until police solved these cases, they'd still be housebound to this day. These cases, along with far too many others, represent a backlog of unsolved disappearances and murders of women in the province of Alberta.

～

According to news reports, on the evening of February 7, 1987, divorcee Susie Kaminsky, 34, and her friend Linda King had stopped at the Rosslyn Motor Inn's Northgate Pub in Edmonton for a couple of drinks.

As the two women talked, Kaminsky noticed a young man she thought she recognized. The 23-year-old man, Roy Sobotiak, was visiting his mother Donalda, a waitress at the pub. Kaminsky remembered babysitting Roy years earlier. The foursome chatted until the bar closed, and Donalda invited Kaminsky and Linda to her home for a few games of pool.

Kaminsky was game, but Linda wasn't impressed with the young man who was reportedly "living on welfare." He gave Linda a "creepy" feeling that she couldn't shake.

After dropping Linda off at her apartment, Kaminsky went to the Sobotiak home where she and the Sobotiaks talked until about 5:00 AM, when Donalda went to bed. Kaminsky and Roy went downstairs to play pool before Kaminsky called it a night and went home to her two children.

That's when everything went terribly wrong.

Police suspected Roy in Kaminsky's disappearance early on in the investigation. But it took more than a year before the investigators got the proof they needed to arrest and finally convict the man of sexual assault and second-degree murder. Kaminsky's body has never been found, though, which still leaves a mystery in this case.

Second Disappearance in One Week

As police were earnestly looking for leads in the Kaminsky case, another young Edmonton woman mysteriously disappeared.

Twenty-four-year-old Melissa Letain was a hairdresser in a West Edmonton Mall salon. She worked the evening shift on Friday, February 13, 1987, and the shop was no doubt busy with women wanting to look their best before celebrating Valentine's Day with their sweethearts.

At 9:10 PM it was dark and chilly when Melissa clocked out from work. She lived only five blocks from the mall, so despite the hour, she opted to walk home.

That choice proved to be a fatal mistake.

According to several newspaper accounts of the story, Letain was last seen walking down a dimly lit walkway "south of 87th Avenue between 175th and 178th Streets." Later updates revealed that in preparation for the next day's Valentine's celebrations, Letain was carrying "a rose, a card, and pennant in a plastic bag," gifts for her boyfriend.

In 1989, RCMP sergeant Del Huget, who was head of K-division's homicide unit, told reporters from the *Edmonton Journal* that among the more than 60 tips that a freshly organized task force was examining, officers were particularly interested in a clue from one witness who said they "saw Letain struggling with a man."

It's not clear when the unnamed witness came forward with concerns; he or she may have even reported the attack before anyone knew Letain had disappeared. Regardless, the woman's attacker was described as "six feet tall, with dark hair, swept at the sides…he had a slim or medium build" and was "wearing a two-tone jacket and dark pants at the time of the attack." The attacker made eye contact with the witness before allegedly dragging Melissa's limp body down the walkway and into a nearby vehicle.

Despite the report from this witness, the police officers who first arrived at the scene didn't feel they had any evidence to back the witness statement. They did, however, find a rose, a card and a pennant. The authorities later recognized the importance of these items. But as *Edmonton Journal* writer Greg Owens pointed out in a 1993 article, police at the scene back then treated the items as litter and had tossed them into a nearby garbage can.

On Valentine's Day, while lovers everywhere were showing their affection for one another, Letain's boyfriend would discover his girlfriend had been brutally taken from him. Letain's body was discovered sprawled on the ice underneath the "Genesee Bridge, 75 km southwest of Edmonton." A group of students out on a snowshoeing trip reported finding the woman's body. In a 2012 newspaper series reviewing some of Edmonton's unsolved murders, one of those students shared his memories of that day, saying they've never really dimmed in his mind. He told the *Edmonton Sun* that a scattering of items, which included pantyhose tied to a yellow rope, surrounded the woman's lifeless body—it was a scene he would never forget.

The murderer no doubt expected Letain's dead weight would have broken through the soft ice—indeed, the student who spoke with the press in 2012 explained how he and his adult chaperone tried to crawl out on the ice to check on the woman but found the "ice was too soft." Miraculously for Letain's loved ones, her body didn't break through the ice; discovering the body wouldn't bring her back, but it afforded her family and friends a measure of closure.

Investigators are guarded about releasing any evidence related to Letain's murder, but over the decades, additional information has been released from time to time in the hope that those details might jar someone's memory. Some of Letain's personal items were recovered, but others—such as a "CN trucking key chain with a single key, a woman's watch, a blue leather or leather-looking woman's wallet and a green clutch purse with a gold clasp"—were never found.

Early on in the investigation it was determined that although Letain hadn't been sexually assaulted, her murder was a particularly violent one and contained sexual undertones. In May 1987, the *Montreal Gazette* explained that Letain was "strangled with a rope, fashioned into a hangman's noose, used in combination with pantyhose." It was the first time in this country that the authorities had seen a crime scene where a hangman's noose was used; most investigators agreed this was a particularly interesting detail in the murder. They also discovered the rope used in the crime "was manufactured in Saskatoon by a company that [had] been out of business for 10 years." The rope wasn't new; it was obvious it had been used in the past. In 1993, *Edmonton Journal* reporter Greg Owens described the rope as "1/4-inch, four-strand yellow polypropylene…[about]…four to five feet in length, with yellow plastic around each of the strands." Because of these unique qualities of the rope, police were hoping that by releasing a detailed description of the rope, someone might remember seeing it.

Although Letain hadn't been raped, psychologists and criminal profilers throughout the years haven't shied away from painting the murderer as a "sexually-motivated psychopath with a rope fetish." They also suggest that the perpetrator may have committed similar assaults in the past and could perhaps commit the same type of crime again—although the use of a hangman's noose in other rape and murder cases hasn't been publicly documented to date. Investigators also uniformly suggested that the murderer would have been "big time proud" of his conquest, but because he was most likely considered a "boy-next-door type" or someone who was a bit on the socially awkward side, anyone he bragged to wouldn't necessarily believe him.

In 1989, police confirmed they had "a number of possible suspects" in Letain's murder, but, to date, an arrest has yet to be made. Because the crime appears to be an isolated incident, is it possible that the person responsible knew the young woman?

In 1997, about 50 DNA samples taken from items gathered from various stages of the investigation into Letain's death were awaiting testing at the RCMP crime lab in Ottawa. No definitive results have managed to help the authorities find the murderer.

Letain's senseless murder continues to haunt the officers involved in the investigation as much today as it had haunted Edmonton residents in 1987.

Headlines Announce Another Missing Woman

Two missing women and a murder discovered within a week's time kept Edmontonians glued to their televisions and devouring their newspapers. But when a third woman, Marcia Charette, disappeared, public anxiety was turning to panic. Was it indeed possible a serial killer was in their midst?

Tuesday, March 24, 1987, was a cold and cloudy day, made grimmer for the Charette family when they discovered they couldn't locate one of their own. Twenty-three-year-old

Marcia Charette had been through the ringer over the previous year. The neo-natal intensive care nurse had accidentally injected an infant with a fatal dose of Paraldehyde—20-times greater than the dose prescribed. The incident was blamed on the "improper labeling of a vial of the drug," but that likely didn't soften the pain for anyone involved, including Marcia.

One can't begin to imagine the possible scenarios that must have floated through the minds of her worried family and friends when they couldn't contact Marcia. But two days after her reported disappearance, Marcia's body was discovered in the trunk of her abandoned Ford Maverick. She had been strangled.

With two strangled women in such a short time, newspaper headlines across the country were boldly voicing the public's fear about the possibility of a serial killer on the loose. "Fear grips Edmonton following murders…" the *Montreal Gazette* announced. "Serial killer feared loose in Edmonton" the *Vancouver Sun* chimed in. As it turned out, Charette's murder was quickly resolved. Not long after her body was discovered, her future brother-in-law was charged and convicted in her strangulation death. The psychology behind why he chose to sacrifice a future with the woman he purportedly loved and savagely attack her sister is something that will always defy explanation.

Solving Charette's homicide was small comfort in a city where several unsolved murders of women were still on the books. Residents were beginning to think that some people were getting away with murder, and the murder of Melodie Riegel, which occurred just a few months earlier, also fed the initial idea that a serial killer was on the loose.

Dangers on the Street

Melodie Riegel, 19, purportedly lived a high-risk (albeit undercover) lifestyle for a part of her life when her body was discovered in an Edmonton hotel on September 21, 1986. Twenty-five years after her body was discovered, the chambermaid who found Melodie told reporters she's still disturbed by what she stumbled upon in the commission of her daily duties. "I was shocked. You could see she was dead because she was blue," the woman who went by the name of "Irene" told *Edmonton Sun*'s Pamela Roth in 2011.

Investigators uncovered several clues in the hours immediately following the discovery of Melodie's body. Melodie had also been strangled. Officers learned that she went by the name of "Tasha" when she was on the streets and had been working the area of 107 Street and 102 Avenue the night she died. The hotel's front desk staff also provided officers with the name of Brent Stevens of Grande Prairie as the individual who booked the room. Police searched in vain for the man who was thought to have been driving a "light-blue half-ton truck parked at the motel on the night Riegel died." It was soon clear the man had provided hotel staff with a false identity; neither he nor his truck were ever found.

More than 25 years have passed, and Melodie's family still mourn their loss. They hadn't known that the petite young woman with the blonde locks and a flare for style had been working the streets. But it doesn't matter what Melodie was doing—no one deserves to die that way. All that matters is that someone will eventually be able to identify her killer, and that the individual is held responsible for the crime.

Edmonton Police Service Acting Detective Bryce Clarke still believes justice is possible. "It only takes one tip to lead us down a different investigative avenue that we haven't pursued before," he told media during a news conference on September 22, 2011. But until officials are certain they have an ironclad case, they will continue to keep some key "pieces of evidence close to [their] chest."

Flashback to 1976

Seventeen-year-old Marie Goudreau had just graduated high school and had big plans for her future. She was working at a coffee shop in Southgate Mall for the summer and was excited about going to university and pursuing a career in social work. Her brother Daniel described his younger sister as beautiful and vivacious with a heart for helping people.

That promising life was cut short on the night of August 2, 1976.

Police believe that Marie stopped her car to help someone near the town of Beaumont by the intersection of RR 244 and Township Road 510—at that time it was a rural road but today it's known as Ellerslie Road. Marie stopped her car sometime between 10:50 and 11:10 PM; investigators knew this because she had stopped by a friend's house before finally making her way home from work that day.

Officers found Marie's car shortly after she was reported missing. The car was parked diagonally, in a haphazard manner, and the headlights were on and the motor left running.

Marie's purse, with $20 in it, was on the front seat, along with her jacket and shoes. Since Marie wasn't known to pick up hitchhikers despite her propensity for helping people, police suspect she had stopped to help someone she would have thought was "friendly." Two worry-filled days lapsed for the family before Marie's nude body was discovered "in a water-filled ditch about three kilometres north of Devon."

Marie's death took place 10 years before the three Edmonton women disappeared in seven short weeks in the spring of 1987, but their disappearance couldn't help but echo Marie's murder—she too had been strangled.

"We thought [Marie's murder] would be solved soon, and we were hoping it would have been," Daniel Goudreau told *Edmonton Sun* reporter Pamela Roth, reflecting back in December 2012 on his sister's case. "You are always thinking some person is maybe doing this again, and you certainly don't want that to happen. It's one of those nagging feelings that you just don't know how to handle."

In the years since Marie's death, investigators have uncovered new information. They've also publicly named two persons of interest in the case: Brett Morgan and Gary McAstocker.

In 1998, Brett Morgan was living in Ottawa when he was convicted of the first-degree murder of 46-year-old Louise Ellis. The woman was a freelance writer who was "interested in justice issues" and had met Morgan when she "heard him testify at a Supreme Court hearing into the wrongful conviction of David Milgaard." Ellis fell in love with Morgan, and she eventually lobbied on his behalf for an early release during his incarceration for what was initially referred to as robbery and fraud.

Morgan moved in with Ellis when he was released in May 1994, but the affection between the two soured quickly. Following Ellis' disappearance on April 22, 1995, suspicion quickly turned to her common-law husband. Morgan's most recent jail stint was pretty common knowledge among Ellis' friends and family, but it wasn't long before media watchdogs covering the case shed additional light on Morgan's past. They learned that Morgan had also been serving time for the 1981 manslaughter of an Edmonton woman when he and Ellis met. A news report from the *Globe and Mail* on September 14, 1981, explained that in 1978, Morgan strangled 21-year-old Edmontonian Gwen Telford "after an evening of drinking."

As it turned out, Morgan's name was also being tossed around as a suspect in the death of 33-year-old Roland Wagstaff after his Edmonton jewellery store was robbed in October 1978, as well as the murder of Marie Goudreau.

The other possible suspect in Goudreau's murder case was Gary McAstocker, a man who'd been convicted twice of rape and sexual assault. Unfortunately, police were never able to question McAstocker about Marie's rape and murder because he died after trying to hang himself before he could be interviewed about a missing youth, 14-year-old Tina McPhee. McPhee was friends with McAstocker's stepchild, and police were eyeing McAstocker as a possible suspect in Tina's disappearance.

Investigators started looking at McAstocker as someone they wanted to question with regard to the Goudreau case before McPhee's disappearance in June 1994. McAstocker's family members had approached Leduc RCMP with concerns that the man may have been involved in "other unsolved crimes." Fearing for their own safety, those family members came forward after McAstocker was released from jail in February 1994.

One of the unsolved crimes the family members suggested McAstocker could have been involved with was the murder of Goudreau. In the year that Goudreau went missing, McAstocker was days away from his 17th birthday. If Marie had happened upon the young man on the roadside looking like he needed help, she may not have felt any threat in the situation because he was another young person like herself.

After Goudreau's murder, stories circulated around the Beaumont-Leduc area about a man following women in their vehicles and posing as a police officer while trying to force his way inside. Could this man have been McAstocker? Or was another predator prowling the rural county?

Suspicions past or current aside, McAstocker had a criminal record that included serious offences, and yet his wife Rita never wavered in her support of him. She told reporters that her husband was a kind man, and although he'd committed heinous crimes, he was upfront with her about them. They were in the past, she argued; he was honest and trustworthy now.

Many months after McAstocker's death in 1994, forensic tests on a skull and pubic hairs recovered from his 1983 brown Datsun pickup confirmed what police had suspected all along. "These test results further substantiate our belief that

Gary McAstocker was responsible for the murder of Tina McPhee," police spokesperson Sergeant Nigel Stevens told the *Edmonton Journal* in December 1995. It was obvious to the more objective investigators that Rita McAstocker's understanding of her husband was coloured by her misguided love for him.

One case was closed, but others remained unsolved. McAstocker was believed to have connections to at least one of the several missing and murdered women the city of Calgary has reported over the years.

Nineteen-year-old Barbara Jean MacLean was discovered north of 90th Avenue and 6th Street N.E. Calgary in a neighbourhood frequently referred to as a "Lovers' Lane" on February 26, 1977. Like Marie Goudreau, Barbara Jean had been strangled.

Gary McAstocker was a suspect in MacLean's murder because he was in Calgary working for an Edmonton-based moving company at the time of her death. Employees from the company typically stayed at the Highlander Motor Hotel when they passed through Calgary. MacLean was last seen at that hotel's parking lot looking for a ride home after having a fight with her boyfriend in the hotel's bar. Was it possible that McAstocker, posing as a concerned citizen having witnessed the argument, had offered MacLean a ride home and then attacked the girl?

Although police hadn't narrowed their investigation to solely focus on McAstocker, Calgary RCMP constable Ed Turco told Rick Mofina of the *Calgary Herald* that the MacLean and

Goudreau murders had several similarities. Both girls were about the same age and "type." Both were sexually assaulted and strangled. Investigators also believed that whoever killed Barbara Jean MacLean was responsible for the murder of a 20-year-old chambermaid Melissa Ann Rehorek, whose body was discovered outside Calgary on September 16, 1976. In 1977, DNA uncovered in the MacLean case was being compared with McAstocker. Further information has not been released to the public, perhaps because McAstocker died before he could go to trial. However, most consider the case of Tina McPhee to be solved.

No End to Sad News

The unsolved cases mentioned in this chapter represent only a small number of murders that have occurred in Alberta over the province's history where the perpetrator remains at large. As often as time and their caseloads allow, investigators review notes and re-examine evidence in the hope that new eyes might notice small details that could bring the murderers to justice. The cases are also revisited every few years in the pages of the local media in the cities where the crimes occurred, hoping that public awareness might jog someone's memory and unearth a new clue.

Theories that a serial killer, or several serial killers, could be responsible for the unsolved murders of these women are still bandied about from time to time. The bodies of Jennifer Joyes, 17; Jennifer Janz, 16; and Keely Pincott, 29, were each discovered in separate shallow graves just outside of Calgary in the summer of 1991; their murders have yet to be solved. Were they victims of a serial killer who plied his sick trade undeterred until his own death put an end to his exploits? Or is their killer still enjoying an unrestricted life and stalking other potential victims with no care for the consequences and no worry that he might get caught?

"In many of these cases, the guy just goes ahead and he does it," Corporal Brian Roberts, head crime analyst for Alberta RCMP told the *Edmonton Journal* in September 1994 during a review of several cases. "It doesn't matter wherever the witnesses are because he is so driven by his fantasy that everything else is excluded."

Although a serial killer might be responsible for some of these homicides, it's doubtful that one person could have committed all of Alberta's unsolved murders. Time and space sometimes separates cases too widely, while other circumstances confuse the evidence and point to yet another, unknown perpetrator, making it doubly disconcerting to think that several dangerous individuals could be roaming freely among us at any given time, possibly looking for their next target.

Whether Gary McAstocker or Brett Morgan were involved with any other crimes than the ones they were convicted of is a mystery that has followed each man to his grave. McAstocker died from the injuries he incurred when he hung himself; Morgan died of hepatitis C while in prison.

Exactly why these women had to die at the hands of an unscrupulous criminal defies explanation. Their stories provide a small glimpse into the mysteries behind unsolved murders in Alberta.

Chapter Thirteen

The Murder of Gary Meier

~

Everything seemed eerily quiet the morning Steve Manoc walked up the steps of Gary Meier's home. Manoc had been there many times in the past, but this was most likely the first time he had to check on his boss after he didn't show up to work earlier that morning. He hadn't shown up the day before either, and since no one could seem to contact him by phone, Manoc decided to check on the man.

The electronic gate at the top of Meier's driveway, which was usually secured, was open and allowed his shop foreman to drive up to the house. Manoc rapped on the front door. No answer.

Manoc tried the door handle, only to find it locked. The back door was locked too, but the door to the attached garage was open, and Manoc decided to enter the house through the garage. No doubt Manoc's decision made him nervous—Meier wasn't the kind of man you just walked in on, uninvited. Still, it wasn't like Meier to miss work. And it definitely wasn't like him not call in to let everyone know what he was up to.

Maybe Meier had a heart attack? Maybe he was sick and needed help? It would take something extreme and unforeseen to prevent the man from keeping his business obligations. No, like it or not, Manoc was going into the house. If everything was okay, and Meier was angry at his boldness, he'd just have to brace himself for Meier's reprimand.

But Meier was not okay. And Manoc was not prepared for what he discovered.

~

It was a hot August evening, and Gary Meier was pulling a late night sitting at his kitchen table and mulling over paperwork, where he was most weekday evenings. The 52-year-old self-made man had achieved his success through a lot of hard work. And although he only had an elementary education, Meier possessed a considerable amount of natural business acumen, which was clearly evident by his financial portfolio; one didn't accumulate a self-worth of more than $5 million without a whole lot of smarts.

The Lacombe businessman made the majority of his money selling and leasing commercial trailers. News stories about Meier have described him as "shrewd," "eccentric" and "notoriously cheap." Others who knew him might have added the descriptors "difficult," "demanding" and even "severe." Regardless of how people felt about the man, few would argue anyone deserved his fate.

News reports telling of how Manoc walked into Meier's home at around 9:30 on the morning of August 10, 2001, are necessarily sterile. The Alberta edition of the now defunct United Western Communications' *Report Newsmagazine* wrote that Manoc "called police after finding his boss dead, slumped over the kitchen table, in Meier's home."

There was blood. Police called to the scene also found bullet holes in the kitchen window, leading them to initially think Meier had been killed from someone outside. The locked entrance doors to the house seemed to support that suggestion. However, once the crime scene was analyzed in more detail, the theory of an outside shooter was dismissed. Instead, it was starting to look like Meier was killed in his own home, quite possibly by someone sitting across the table from him.

If that was the case, since there was no sign of forced entry anywhere in the house, it suggested that Gary Meier's murderer was someone he knew and someone he wasn't afraid of.

And that fact could potentially open up a huge list of suspects in the homicide of Gary Meier.

Victim Profile

In 2011, Statistics Canada reported that "homicide is a relatively rare offence in Canada, representing less than one percent of all crimes." The report further explains that "three-quarters (76 percent) of all homicides in 2011 were solved by police," and "the majority of homicides (70 percent) are solved within one week." Furthermore, an acquaintance, a friend or a business associate of the victim commits most homicides. This is one statistic that has remained constant throughout the years, regardless of the location of the murder. Investigators quickly honed in on several suspects that could fit that description in the murder of Gary Meier.

Meier had a lot going on in his life. After all, running a profitable business can, in itself, open a person up to potential conflict. But it wasn't Meier's business dealings that caught the attention of police and journalists alike early on in the investigation. And his selling and leasing of commercial trailers didn't interest authorities either.

Meier and his wife, Lori, were estranged. Lori was living in Calgary with the couple's two children, but the distance separating their two residences hadn't done much to ease the couple's tension. In fact, Lori had a restraining order against her soon-to-be ex-husband.

Gary was probably frustrated over the marital breakdown as well, especially since it was reportedly costing him several thousands of dollars every month for spousal and child support. And his alleged girlfriend in nearby Bentley must have cost him money too. According to the *Report* story, Meier was "planning to leave the country in September." Although specific details weren't stated, it was suggested that Meir would be gone for a considerable length of time, and the girlfriend was supposedly going to join him later that month.

Police tend to want to rule out spouses and significant others first when investigating a murder. That Lori might have hired someone to kill Gary was bandied about among his friends and family members; after all, they certainly battled with Lori in court for years over the rightful control of the man's estate after Gary's death. But Lori was her own best advocate—she posted a $50,000 reward for information leading to an arrest of the person or persons responsible for her estranged husband's death. She also established a website about the murder, which included "descriptions of the last individuals believed to have seen him alive." It seemed she wanted to get some answers to clear her own name and give her children some closure.

The Crime Scene

It was originally believed that Gary was killed by the hail of bullets that penetrated the window near the kitchen table where he sat. But there were holes in that theory, such as the drawn blinds, which would make it impossible for any marksman to have a clear view of his or her target. Another problem was the gunshot wound that killed the businessman. Investigators toyed with the theory that Gary had been sitting at the kitchen table, with his murderer sitting in front of him. Based on the trajectory of that bullet, however, the angle couldn't support that theory. The bullet that killed Gary "would have penetrated the neck and shoulder area, passing out through the stomach and groin." This evidence suggested the murderer had stood behind the victim.

A closer look at the crime scene raised another question. Where were the blood splatter patterns investigators would expect to find in either of these scenarios? If someone sitting in front of Gary shot him, there'd be a spray of blood on the wall behind him. The blood at the crime scene didn't support some-one coming up from behind the man either, and police wondered whether Gary might have been killed elsewhere and his body later moved to the kitchen. They also wondered if more than one killer was involved, especially since two guns were used: the bullets that came through Meier's kitchen window and the single bullet that killed him had come from two different guns.

Although the theories shed some light on *how* Gary Meier was killed, they didn't point to a suspect or provide a motive.

Lori's decision to hire Calgary-based detective Bruce Dunne, a one-time police officer turned private investigator, unearthed a few disturbing surprises. While Lori was busy doing her part to help solve the case by maintaining her website, Dunne came across a witness who had an unusual story to share. If that informant was correct, Gary may have inadvertently laid the groundwork for his own murder.

Motive Behind the Murder

According to Dunne, Gary had made friends with a group of bikers, flashed a few bills in their direction and promised a hefty payday should they do what he asked.

And what he allegedly asked was a monumental request.

"Gary had promised to pay [the members of a biker gang] $20,000 to kill his estranged wife and her divorce lawyer," Dunne said to Lisa Joy of the *Lacombe Globe* in 2012.

The story goes that Gary made a $2000 down payment to two different bikers in June 2001; they'd get the rest of the money once their services had been rendered. Dunne believed that when they couldn't find Lori and dispose of her as requested, these bikers still wanted Gary to pay the rest of the money he'd promised them. This clearly wouldn't sit well with a savvy businessman like Gary. Being the self-assured person he was, he probably didn't blink an eye at the threat they posed when he refused to pay what they asked.

If so, his bravado was a fatal mistake.

There was another possible motive for Meier's murder; it could have been planned all along. If Meier did contract someone to murder his estranged wife and her lawyer, the killers would have done their homework and researched their employer. They would have known he kept a lot of money on his person and in his home—a widely known fact. As well, witnesses interviewed after Meier's body was discovered told police the man showed them a $250,000 Bank Bearer Bond and $70,000 in cash just days earlier. And yet when police searched Meier's home, they didn't find the bond.

While Dunne stood by his biker theory as recently as 2012, police involved in the case have officially discarded the theory. According to the *Lacombe Globe*, police have followed up on more than 400 tips. They added that Meier had difficult relationships with several people, suggesting the list of suspects is longer than the two bikers Dunne fingered in this case.

More than a decade has passed since Gary Meier was murdered. His estate was eventually settled, with a large portion of it going to Lori. Although the matters of money and property have been cleared away, the mystery surrounding Meier's demise extend far beyond his death. Did he really plan to leave the country with his girlfriend? Was Meier the kind of man who would seriously consider hiring a hit man to get rid of his wife and her lawyer? Did he know the person or persons who executed him that August night?

While the answers to these questions are unknown, one thing is certain. Gary Meier's murderers will have to look over their shoulders for the rest of their lives. This cold case is never far from the minds of investigators in Red Deer. People in Lacombe have not forgotten. And Gary's family will not rest until his killer or killers are brought to justice.

MANUFACTURED
MYSTERIES

Chapter Fourteen

Company Town: The Atlas Coal Mine

~

It's more than 30°C outside. On hot summer days like these, I'm happy to be pulling coal for the Atlas Coal Mine. Even though the work is hard, the tunnels are cool. The warmest spots are half the temperature of that above ground, so although we sweat, we've got it better than the men doing yard maintenance or the poor fellow in the blacksmith shop.

Money's better too. We're pretty lucky here. The lads working at other sites are lucky if they get a roof, some grub and credit at the company store for putting their lives on the line every time they go underground. Here, we get cash for our efforts most times. Of course, who couldn't do with a little more jingle in the jeans—there's often talk about organizing the men and demanding more pay, but I don't complain. Those who complain too much sometimes find themselves out of work.

The wife's not keen on my working inside the mine though. After the last two men plummeted to their deaths on their way home from work, she begged me to work on the tipple, maintaining the machines—anything other than disappearing into the darkness for another shift. She even suggested I take up farming. Imagine that! Work just as hard for half the pay. I say no to that.

We've got two little ones to feed and clothe, and now there's another on the way this spring, just in time for layoffs. If I don't get a guarantee they'll take me back after shutdown, I might have to put on some big boy pants and get a steady job after all. The wife would like that. Me...I'd miss the mine.

~

Some might argue that the biggest mystery at the Atlas Coal Mine near Drumheller in any given year was if the employees would have jobs in the coming season, and if they did, whether they'd get paid as they had in years past or just be provided with room and board and credits at the company store.

Folks today might suggest a far bigger enigma was why these men returned to the mine, year after year, knowing they might be turned away with nothing more than their sleeping rolls and whatever grub they snagged from the coyotes hunting the fields where they lay their heads at night.

The truth was that starting a fresh life in a new and promising land was better than what many of these men could hope for back home. Russians, Poles, Ukrainians, Hungarians, Romanians, Italians—the men willing to work in the mines immigrated to this part of Canada from so many countries that a visit to the local pub on payday was like a roundtable at the United Nations. But beyond the hope for a brighter future, something about the mining life was like no other. The camaraderie between the men couldn't be found anywhere else; one's life often depended on how well the men worked together. That camaraderie was pretty strong at the Atlas Coal Mine.

The Atlas Coal Mine wasn't the first coal mine to open its doors in the Drumheller Valley. The Newcastle Mine earned that honour when it hauled its first load of coal out of the

Some say the ghosts of former mine workers continue to toil within the Atlas Coal Mine's wooden tipple. The mine is the last of its kind still standing in Canada.

neighbouring hillsides in 1911, but Atlas wasn't far behind, opening for business in 1917. Not to be outdone, Atlas, located just outside of East Coulee, earned accolades of its own as the last coal mine of the 139 mines to pull coal from Drumheller's hillsides. Atlas closed its doors when its last shaft, the Atlas #4, ceased production on December 10, 1979.

Working in a coal mine was both dirty and dangerous, but Drumheller's fields were known as "sub-bitumous," which was an ideal source for heating, cooking and generating electricity. Because sub-bitumous coal is "immature," it doesn't expel the high concentrations of methane gas found in other, more mature coal mines. Although the Atlas Mine had experienced a methane explosion a time or two over the course of its history, accidents were rare. The safety record definitely added to the lure of mining in that particular part of Alberta.

But despite the Atlas Coal Mine boasting that it never had a major disaster as part of its work history, 16 men met their deaths doing their jobs over the company's 62 years in production. And there are people who believe the spirits of some of those men inhabit the mine to this day.

Brothers Grim

Twenty-seven-year-old Robert Ole Myers and his brother John, 32, are among the apparitions that some visitors with psychic abilities believe still roam the shafts of Atlas #4. The brothers were tired but excited to head home after a long, hard day underground. At around 11:40 on the night of Friday, January 19, 1962, they called the hoist operator and asked to be raised to the surface. The hoist operator slowly released the brake, and the men could feel themselves making their way to ground level.

It's ironic how a person can be exhausted and yet, when it's quitting time, get a mental second wind and start plotting off-duty activities. John might have been thinking about his two little boys—more than likely they would want some attention that weekend. Robert was single, so perhaps the young man was planning for a night on the town.

The hoist was so near the surface it's quite conceivable that the two passengers on board may have made eye contact with the operator just before the unthinkable happened. A hair of a second later, John and Robert's plans for some rest and relaxation were forever altered.

"The brake would not hold and the lift broke away, slamming to the surface," the operator later testified regarding the incident. Mine manager Hugh Crawford estimated the lift climbed at a speed of about 4 miles (6 kilometres) per hour. When the brake gave way, the fall would have been considerably faster—Crawford estimated the descent would have clocked 70 miles (112 kilometres) per hour by the time it hit the bottom, 400 feet (120 metres) below.

John and Robert were killed in the accident, and a post mortem "showed both victims sustained a tremendous number of fractures, lacerations and brain damage." The accident so traumatized the hoist operator that he had to be hospitalized.

Shock, sadness and outrage enveloped the mining community of East Coulee and the surrounding area. The rally cry coming from the people suggested mine management was responsible for the accident. Machines like the hoist should have been maintained better, and management should have invested more money in ensuring the safety of their employees, some residents argued. Management, on the other hand, argued that the accident was simply that, a tragic accident. After hearing the

Stories of ghostly encounters at the Atlas Coal Mine are so plentiful that several groups of paranormal professionals have visited the site to research the claims.

~

evidence presented at the inquiry into the accident, a "six-man jury deliberated for 35 minutes before returning with the verdict of death resulting at the bottom of the shaft as a result of the failure of the braking system by reasons not presented in the testimonies." For all intents and purposes, the mining company had been absolved of any responsibility in the incident.

This conclusion, according to some psychics, didn't sit well with the Myers brothers.

Spirit Stalkers

"One group of professional mediums sensed a lot of ghostly activity in the mine office," explained Jaffra Markotic, a tour guide of the Atlas Coal Mine Society. The Atlas Coal Mine was designated a National Historic Site of Canada in 1989 and its buildings and contents turned over to the care of the Atlas Coal Mine Society. Markotic is one of several tour guides regaling tourists with tales of Alberta's early history in that corner of the province. Each guide has a specialty or two, and one of Markotic's areas of expertise is conducting the site's weekly ghost tours. One of the stories he tells is connected to the tragic deaths of the Myers brothers.

Markotic explained that one group of mediums visiting the site sensed the presence of a tall, skinny man dressed in casual clothes lounging in the mine office, with his feet propped up on the desk. He was talking in an Eastern European accent to a heavy-set man who was smoking a pipe and leaning up against the office safe. The psychics suggested the heavy-set man appeared to be the boss, but he had a kindly disposition. The other man was, they believed, one of the miners. The two were having a discussion that appeared to involve some kind of mine accident, and the boss said he had "handled it as best as he could," and that it was "best to let the documents be in the safe."

The story didn't ring true to the mine staff who heard it. "It just seemed unlikely [that the manager would be discussing anything with a miner] because of the tension between miners and management," Markotic said, explaining how at the time, management and miners went out of their way to ensure they didn't live in the same part of town.

On another occasion, an intuitive visitor to the mine also sensed something in the mine office. This woman said the impressions she was getting focused on miners she believed were accident victims. "She said it would be better for the families to let the miners rest for now," Markotic said.

Staff at the mine often research claims of sightings, whether they come from professional paranormal researchers or self-professed psychics, especially when there are striking similarities or overlaps between stories. One reason staff investigate these claims might be the sheer number of experiences various staff members themselves have reported over the years. Although Markotic hasn't had any ghostly encounters himself, some of his colleagues have reported seeing ghosts or witnessing "spooky things," especially in the washhouse, which is purported to be one of the "most haunted buildings" on site. The claims made of a "boss" and "miner" having a chat in the office, and the spirits of accident victims hanging out there, prompted museum

management to investigate the possibilities that these percep-
tions might, indeed, be grounded in fact.

Surprisingly, there seemed to be a connection between the
psychics' readings of the office and the mine's history. When
the mediums involved in the above story looked through old
photos, they pointed out two men: one was the manager in 1962
during the time the Myers brothers met their untimely demise,
and the other was a miner on staff at that same time. It was confirmed that the two men were friends, and furthermore, those
men represented the only two possibilities to fit the descriptions
provided by the first group of paranormal researchers. This con-
firmation also fit nicely with another psychic who sensed the
presence of the spirits of accident victims in the office as well,
though she did not tie her insight to any particular miners.

Could it be that the public outcry in 1962 suggesting that
management neglect was responsible for at least some of the accidents at the Atlas Coal Mine had some merit? And is it possible
that the spirits of mortally injured miners still stalk the one-time
mining office to this day, looking for justice?

Coincidence or Camouflage?

If you're not inclined to believe in ghosts, a more concrete mystery is connected to the experiences reported at the
mine office—a mystery that some mediums have suggested adds
another bizarre twist to the controversy surrounding the deaths
of the Myers brothers.

The unique physical properties of the Atlas Coal Mine make it an interactive museum of paramount importance. If they allowed their imaginations to have full rein, visitors will experience as intimate a view of history as possible without having actually lived at that time; a priceless gift, most would agree. When Century Coals, the company who owned the Atlas Mine, turned over the buildings and their contents to the care of the Atlas Coal Mine Historical Society, two main components of the mine weren't initially part of that deal: the key to the door to the mine office and the combination to the office safe located inside. Exactly why the owners wanted to keep the mine office and its contents out of bounds for historians and visitors wasn't explained. It was, however, interesting to note that the manager in 1962 had kept his office door locked at all times during his tenure at the mine. Was this just a continuation of past practices, one might question?

Several years after the society took control of the lands, vandals broke into the mine office and, as luck would have it, let themselves out the front door. Now the building was no longer locked, so society members approached the mine's original owners to suggest that this might be a good time to keep that building open to the public as well.

"The owners agreed. In fact, they couldn't really remember why they hadn't handed over the keys to the office in the first place," Markotic said.

There was still the problem of the locked safe, however. The mine's previous owners didn't have a record of the combination to the safe, and they didn't appear to be in any hurry to discover a way to open it without doing irreparable and devaluing damage to the artifact. Taking matters into their own hands, museum staff called up one of the secretaries who had worked at the mine. Try as she might, though, she couldn't remember the combination.

Many tools and supplies remain scattered throughout the Atlas Coal Mine's work yard.

"There's still no way to get into the safe," Markotic said. "I guess we'll never know what's inside until we find a way to open it without damaging it."

It's unbelievable to think that with today's technology there isn't a way to open this metal lockbox without harming its historical integrity. It's equally strange that no one previously associated with the mine recalls the combination to the safe, and if someone does know the combination, why hasn't this person come forward with an offer to open it? Is it possible that the Myers brothers, and other accident victims, are calling out to the caretakers of this historic site, hoping researchers might finally open that safe and find something incriminating hiding inside its metal walls? Might there be money or gold or some other item of value locked away for safekeeping? Or does the safe sit there, devoid of anything of value?

More Hauntings

The Atlas Coal Mine's ghost tales go beyond the happenings in this intriguing office. Psychics have sensed ghosts lingering at other locations at the site. Markotic's reference to the unexplained auras and strange happenings that have occurred in the company's washhouse have extended beyond staff experiences—mediums have "seen" strange happenings here, too.

"In 2007 a group of professional mediums told us they sensed three ghosts in the washhouse," Markotic said.

"Surprisingly, these were the spirits of three women, and it was illegal for women to work in the mines at that time."

Markotic went on to explain that these women were special; they represented a unique brand of entrepreneurs, so to speak, and they plied their trade among the miners, especially on paydays.

"Some of the women were running their own businesses and were not working in a brothel," Markotic said, referring to the two well-established brothels that operated on the outskirts of Drumheller, as well as the smaller operations that sometimes took root in the neighbouring mining communities. "They would stop by the mine on payday to catch the miners before they went to town."

Sometimes, Markotic added, these women performed their services on credit and sorted out the finer details of payment later. And to stave off any second thoughts a miner might have about committing to the deed, a bed was conveniently located in the attic above the washhouse where these women offered to provide a little womanly comfort to the freshly scrubbed men.

Again, Atlas staff was suspicious of the mediums' suggestions. In fact, they were pretty sure these psychics had it wrong because the bed in the attic was actually used by the night watchman employed by Atlas through the years. But a chance interview with a miner who worked at the site between 1951 and 1956 confirmed the psychics' story. He said there were indeed women who'd plied their trade in the dark and dusty confines of the washhouse attic.

Yet another account by visiting mediums involved the mine's on-site infirmary. Using an EVP recorder (a device that records electronic voice phenomenon), the mediums picked up on the voice of a woman who appeared to be quite knowledgeable when it came to medical matters. This woman was a doctor, according to the psychics, and she was comforting a man with a serious injury.

"The staff actually checked back in the company records and they did find a contract on the hiring of a woman doctor," Markotic said. The doctor's name was Charlotte Jean le Riche, and she was working at the mine in 1961.

Staff, mediums and visitors alike have reported several other phenomena over the years. Difficulty breathing or shortness of breath, dry mouth, a sense of heaviness or feeling the presence of someone standing behind them when no one was there, experiencing cold pockets of air or a sudden hot sweat, sightings of transparent images of people, items inexplicably moved from one location to another, the rapid draining of camera batteries—these are just a handful of the unexplained accounts visitors share with staff season after season.

Although some of the staff who guide visitors through the mine believe the apparitions and strange experiences are proof positive that ghosts are real, others are still skeptical.

"I'm not sure if I believe or not," Markotic said. "It's certainly interesting. But I haven't witnessed anything.

And I supposedly grew up in a house that was haunted, and I never saw anything there either."

On the other hand, Markotic admits that the stories shared by the mediums as well as the follow-up research seem to support the claim that unsettled spirits may be wandering the earth alongside us, searching for some kind of closure to the difficulties they experienced during their earthly lives.

"These mediums over the years, a lot of them have been more accurate than what we initially gave them credit for," Markotic said.

Other Unknowns

Ghost stories at the Atlas Coal Mine office aren't the only unexplained mysteries the historic site has boasted over the years. A more concrete conundrum historians pondered over was the "cartop shed," a small, square, wooden building located near the washhouse. Its location suggested it would have been used as a lamp house, where miners would collect their headlamps before going underground. The problem was that the former miners interviewed about the building said Atlas never had a lamp house—they brought their own carbide lamps to work every day from home and picked up fresh batteries near the mineshaft, a considerable distance away from where the cartop shed was located.

The mystery had staff so befuddled that in 2003, according to a plaque on site, Museums Alberta and AltaGas Utilities united to financially support research into the topic.

After studying aerial photos, conducting additional interviews and going through the contents of the shed, researchers concluded that the building had indeed been a lamp house at one time, but that it came from another of the East Coulee coal mines, the Murray Mine, which closed in 1942. Why the lamp house was moved, who moved it, and when, all remain unclear.

The Atlas Coal Mine harbours other countless mysteries that remain uncovered. Each person connected to the mine—from the miners to the housewives and children, the numerous officials and managers, office staff and maintenance workers—had a story of their own. Many times those stories were mired in intrigue and, like the contents of the locked safe at the Atlas mine office, have been hidden from public view for generations. Like the cowboys roaming the ranchlands when this province was still in its infancy, Alberta's early miners and the people who touched their lives have contributed their fair share to the "wild" in the Wild West of Alberta.

Chapter Fifteen

Classified: Project Habbakuk

~

Patricia Lake is about 5.5 kilometres from downtown Jasper, along Pyramid Lake Road. Named after Queen Victoria's granddaughter, Princess Patricia of Connaught, the long and narrow nugget of a lake is a jewel amid the crown that is the Rocky Mountains, offering visitors the best in wilderness activities that includes a unique underwater adventure.

If you're so inclined, and you're competent enough to venture out on your own, the Alberta Underwater Council suggests several ways of getting to the remote western tip of the southern corner of the lake. Because Pyramid Lake Road pretty much ends at the centre of the lake, near the family-owned Patricia Lake Bungalows, hauling diving gear to the southern shore can be quite the challenge. Adventurers have the option of hoisting a canoe or rowboat onto their vehicles and, with permission from Patricia Lake Bungalow staff, cast off from the boat launch.

Because motors aren't allowed on Patricia Lake, your only option is to paddle to your destination, though it will take you quite some time. A 20-minute scooter ride or a hike along the horse trail will get you there as well, but hauling the heavy diving equipment makes the hike a challenge.

You'll know you've reached your destination when you see a patch of tar along the shore and a metal eyelet, like the kind used to anchor a boat to land. These represent some of the few remains of a top-secret project carried out along the shoreline of Patricia Lake during the heat of World War II.

To see more of this mysterious project, you'll have to don your scuba gear and slowly make your way into the icy depths of the mountain lake. Swimming ever so carefully so as not to disturb the soft glacial silt or rock flour lining the lake's bottom, you'll reach depths of 13 metres before you come across a commemorative plaque installed in 1988 by divers from the Alberta Underwater Archaeology Society. You'll begin to notice odd bits of board or remnants of refrigeration pipes, debris that continues down in an angular direction to about 30 metres. As you review the remains of what was once a ship-like vessel, keep in mind that you are one of a relatively small number of people who know this wreckage exists or the mystery surrounding it.

The ravages of war are always unpredictable, but a few months into World War II, the Atlantic Ocean was already becoming a graveyard for Allied forces. German U-boats (*Unterseeboot;* "undersea boat") travelling undetected underwater were attacking convoys of Allied ships ferrying supplies for the war effort. As stealthy and cunning as the animal these fleets were named after, the Wolf Fleets would sneak up on their prey and attack, leaving their targets stunned and unable to mount an effective defence.

According to *War at Sea: A Naval History of World War II*, penned by Nathan Miller, what Winston Churchill called the "Battle of the Atlantic" occurred in the midst of the North Atlantic shipping routes, and 222 Allied ships were sunk by German U-boats between September and December 1939. As frightening as that statistic was, the number increased by leaps and bounds over the next few years: 1059 ships were downed in 1940; 1299 in 1941; and a staggering 1664 in 1942. By Churchill's own admission, the "U-boat peril" was "the only thing that really frightened [him] during the war." The Allied forces believed that if the world ever wanted to experience peacetime again, it was crucial to manage the damage inflicted on them by the opposing Axis powers.

The Germans knew their U-boats were doing their job. "Once more a red fire blows steeply upwards...the factory will do no more work for Herr Churchill...tomorrow morning Coventry will lie in smoke and ruins." While it's uncertain if this quote should be rightly attributed to German politician Josef Goebbels or to the Reich's Minister of Propaganda, Adolph Hitler himself, or some other source, the quote's sentiment suggests that the Axis had the upper hand in one of the longest fought battles and most deadly battlegrounds of World War II.

The Allied powers, however, weren't going to suffer through these assaults without developing an attack plan of their own.

"We have taken and are taking all possible measures to meet this steady attack. And we are now fighting against it with might and main," Churchill said to the British people during his broadcast address on April 27, 1941. "That is what is called the Battle of the Atlantic which, in order to survive, we have got to win on salt water just as decisively as we had to win the Battle of Britain last August and September in the air."

Churchill was keenly aware that the Allied forces had to organize a new way to fight this ever-growing threat and would require planes and ammunition to do so. The problem was that their planes needed a safe place to land, and the heart of the battlefield was too far from shore for pilots to refuel and return to the watery war zone. The aircraft carriers weren't sufficient for the task. For one thing, there weren't enough of them. For another, they moved slowly. Another issue was that their flight decks were too short for the landing and takeoff requirements of more modern aircraft, and these newer bombers were too large to fit inside the carriers' hangars. Constructing larger hangers would take time, a lot of steel, money and skilled men to do the work involved, all of which were scarce in the thick of war.

Churchill desperately needed to think of a way to deal with the problem.

The Innovations of War

Situations like the ones Churchill faced prompted scientific minds around the world at that time to create newer weapons technologies to target the specific weaknesses encountered in battle. Britain's Royal Navy proposed the development of "midget submarines" that would be less detectable than their full-sized counterparts. The United States suggested the use of Mexican free-tailed bats, which could be strapped onto incendiary devices and dropped by bombers over their targets—a plan that promised to be a suicide mission for the bats with dubious results for the war effort. And American psychologist B.F. Skinner went so far as to suggest that pigeons be placed inside a missile and taught to recognize a target and peck the appropriate lever to detonate the bomb in the missiles.

When Louis Mountbatten, Britain's Chief of Combined Ops, visited Churchill in late 1942, he was told the prime minister was temporarily indisposed and in the bath. It wasn't surprising that he tore up the stairs and barged into the privy because Mountbatten had received a new idea that, if developed, could spell an end to their troubles in the Atlantic. And he could think of no better way to demonstrate that idea than with Churchill in a tub full of water.

A baffled Churchill barely had a moment to utter his objections when Mountbatten tossed a block of ice into Churchill's bath. It melted almost immediately. Mountbatten then tossed in a second, smaller, block of ice that floated on the surface and held its shape. It didn't melt.

Now Mountbatten had Churchill's attention.

What if this "super-ice" were used to produce an aircraft carrier of sufficient size to accommodate World War II bombers, with an airstrip suitable for landing, Mountbatten explained.

And what if this carrier sported a virtually indestructible body that could withstand the most powerful armaments with little to no damage, and what if any damage could be readily repaired with nothing more than the salt water from the sea? If such an ice ship could be constructed, it would no doubt provide the ray of hope the Allied forces needed in the Battle of the Atlantic.

Mountbatten's demonstration boosted Churchill's spirits, and in a formal address he said, "I attach the greatest importance to the examination of these ideas. The advantages of a floating island, or islands, if only used as refueling depots for aircraft, are so dazzling that they do not at the moment need to be discussed."

He also added a caution: "The scheme is only possible if we let nature do nearly all the work for us, and use as raw material seawater and low temperature. The scheme will be destroyed if it involves the movement of very large numbers of men and heavy tonnage of steel or concrete to the remote recesses of the arctic night."

Tragic News Spurs Quest for Answers

The idea for an aircraft carrier constructed mainly of ice was regenerated by an unlikely source.

The RMS *Titanic* was a first-class passenger ship that sported the best of the best for its day. When the ship set sail from Southampton for its maiden voyage on April 10, 1912, with 2224 passengers and crew on board, its trajectory included stops in France and Ireland before heading across the Atlantic to

New York. It was smooth sailing, an enjoyable journey by all accounts, until the ship they said would never sink hit an iceberg about 600 kilometres south of Newfoundland. The collision occurred on April 14 at 11:40 PM. By 2:20 AM, less than three hours later, the Titanic broke apart and foundered. The more than 1000 people that were still on board at that time met their deaths in the frigid waters of the Atlantic Ocean.

Despite the shock and anger that rippled around the world, it was believed that an iceberg of such a mass wasn't something anyone could do much about.

Or could they?

The *Titanic* certainly wasn't the first ship to fall victim to these large ice masses often seen floating off the Grand Banks of Newfoundland since the first explorers set foot on this vast continent. But it wasn't until this tragedy that officials around the world started plotting ways to protect ocean-bound vessels. Was it possible to establish some kind of ice patrol whose main mission would be to blast larger ice flows into smaller, less dangerous ones in the patch of Atlantic known as "Iceberg Alley?" Many years passed between the *Titanic*'s demise and the establishment on June 25, 1936, of the International Ice Observation and Ice Patrol Service, now simply known as the International Ice Patrol, but the effort bore fruit for the war effort in an unexpected way.

The International Ice Patrol's main purpose was to identify and destroy large ice masses that posed a threat to a safe Atlantic crossing. But the patrol quickly discovered that it wasn't possible to blast a large iceberg apart—the most powerful explosion accomplished little more than a small dent in these icy giants of the sea. And efforts to knock the top off one of these big bergs revealed its much larger, underwater portion.

Meanwhile, with each passing day of World War II, more and more lives were claimed. Those losses, coupled with the knowledge of the Ice Patrol, prompted an innovative, albeit eccentric, scientist to approach the problem with an "if you can't beat them, join them" attitude.

The Man Behind the Idea

Geoffrey Nathaniel Joseph Pyke was a well-educated British man who worked as an undercover war correspondent for six days during the initial weeks of World War I before he was captured and imprisoned. Although his cunning didn't keep him from being captured, Pyke's cleverness and smooth manner gained him additional freedoms over time until, almost a year into the war, he escaped from the Ruhleben internment camp where he was being held.

By 1927, Pyke found himself financially destitute, but his mind was as sharp as ever. He was an active pacifist who spoke out publicly against Nazis Germany's stand against Jewish people, among other injustices of the day.

He was also an inventor, and he designed a special motorcycle sidecar to help officers in the Spanish civil war deliver medical aid and supplies to wounded soldiers. Early on in World War II, Pyke invented a screw-propelled vehicle named

A man preparing the ice for the secret Project Habbakuk built in the Rocky Mountains.

~

Operation Plough that acted almost like a snowmobile, helping soldiers cope with deep drifts during winter.

As quirky as many of his inventions were, and although Pyke acquired the unfortunate nickname the "Ozzard of Whizz" by many of his contemporaries, he found an audience in Lord Mountbatten for the invention that prompted him to bust into Churchill's private bath and throw an ice cube in his direction.

And to think it all had to do with icebergs.

An Idea Forms

Because ice is lighter than water and floats, it made sense to use ice as the main structure in a super-sized aircraft carrier capable of receiving the big planes and bombers required to protect Allied supply ships. From an economic point of view, the metal and steel used in traditional aircraft carriers was scarce; ice was plentiful. A vessel made mostly out of ice wouldn't set off any radar alerts and therefore could pass over magnetic mines safely. And if a torpedo did locate and target the ice ship, any damage to its mass could be easily repaired—the readily available seawater would freeze quickly.

In the spring of 1942, Pyke initially considered levelling off the tops of the icebergs to use as floating landing strips, as well as hollowing out these large bergs to house planes and crew on the inside. Several problems with this model included the question of how to capture a floating iceberg and carve it into what Pyke envisioned, not to mention the brittle quality of pure ice, which wouldn't hold up to the abuse it would undergo.

Because ice, by itself, was too brittle to be dependable, Pyke reasoned that adding some kind of substance to the ice would reinforce it and greatly enhance its strength.

Pyke's suggestion was passed on to Herman Mark and Walter Hohenstein, two American scientists who were working out of Brooklyn's Polytechnic Institute's Cold Research Laboratory. Mark and Hohenstein turned their attention to Pyke's proposal to build an aircraft carrier made out of ice. The two scientists experimented with mixing different substances with water and found that rough wood pulp provided a better bonding agent than sawdust or other materials. They further discovered that by freezing a solution of 14 percent wood pulp and

86 percent water they could create a substance that was still as buoyant as straight ice, but as durable as cement.

It was a block of this cement-strength ice that Mountbatten threw into Churchill's bathtub the day he visited in December 1942.

Some academics have suggested the new material, named "pykrete" in honour of Pyke and his ingenuity, should more correctly be described as the rediscovery of a tool used for hundreds of years by the Inuit in building sleds and other structures. Regardless of its true history, pykrete sounded like the solution to an ever-perplexing problem in the war effort.

The Nuts and Bolts

Although sources differ, the full-scale version of Pyke's aircraft carrier could conceivably have measured 1200 metres long, 182 metres wide and 45 metres deep. Pyke claimed that the construction of a bergship the size he'd proposed would require only one percent of the energy needed to construct a similar model made of steel.

The War Illustrated ran a story on Habbakuk on April 12, 1946, just after the war had ended and top-secret projects were being unveiled to the public. The story suggested it was Winston Churchill who code-named Pyke's dream ship project Habbakuk, a misspelled reference to the Old Testament book of Habakkuk. The most common interpretation for this biblical connection refers to God's response to the prophet Habakkuk who questioned the fairness of the good suffering

Workers building the base of Habbakuk.

and of the evil prospering in Habakkuk 1:5: "Look at the nations and watch—and be utterly amazed. For I am going to do something in your days that you would not believe, even if you were told."

Perhaps Churchill felt God's direction in Pyke's plans to build the bergship; in his mind it may have represented an opportunity for the Allied forces to gain an upper hand and possibly right some of the injustices of that horrible war.

Churchill was thrilled when the Canadian government agreed to proceed with their input into this part of the war effort. As the calendar turned, and 1943 dawned, the Canadian contribution to Project Habbakuk began to take shape.

The Canadian Connection

Now that the decision makers within the Allied officials were on board, Pyke's invention moved from the outline stage to the development of a 1/50-scale model. The Canadian official responsible for managing this country's contribution to the war effort, and the top-secret building of a model of the aircraft carrier as envisioned by Pyke, was one Chalmers Jack (C.J.) Mackenzie. Mackenzie was acting president of the National Research Council at the time, and he had his reservations about the project. A 1997 article penned by Bruce Ward, and published in the *Hamilton Spectator*, suggested Mackenzie echoed Prime Minister Mackenzie King's estimation of Project Habbakuk as "another of those mad, wild schemes [that can start] with a couple of crazy men in England and get Churchill's attention and the attention of the highest people in Canada." In Mackenzie's opinion, should the idea have been brought forth in "normal circles" here in Canada, "we should not have the ghost of a chance of getting it before even a minor official."

Nevertheless, Mackenzie was a man who didn't shirk his responsibilities, and by the end of January 1943, he'd contracted the applicable departments at the University of Manitoba, the University of Saskatchewan and the University of Alberta to research everything there was to know about the properties of ice. If he was going to have his name associated with this project, Mackenzie wanted to understand everything he could on the matter.

While the academics were figuring out the science behind the ice monolith, Mackenzie turned his attention to the next step in the process. He needed to decide on a suitably top-secret location to build a prototype of Habbakuk. Earlier in the planning stages, climate was recognized as a major factor in choosing an appropriate setting to build the prototype. Canada and Russia both experience cold winters, and since natural freezing was seen as producing the best results, the climate of both countries was deemed favourable.

Once it was determined that the building of the scale model would occur in Canada, one of the locations Mackenzie looked at was Corner Brook, Newfoundland. Perhaps the most sensible reason for choosing this place over many of the others under review was the region's deep harbour with easy access to the Atlantic Ocean. The downfalls to the Newfoundland location were the lack of available workers and the less private nature of the locale. Churchill, Manitoba, was another contender, but it also was crossed off because the climate was too cold, making it too difficult for the men to work under such conditions.

After examining several locations in which to build the boat, a remote lake in the middle of the Rocky Mountains was finally chosen.

Patricia Lake, a body of water situated at the foot of Pyramid Mountain, was at the time a far more remote location than it is today, and it offered builders the seclusion needed to keep the project on the down low. In addition, while the mountain peaks surrounding the area had long been a huge draw for avid skiers and backcountry enthusiasts, public access had been restricted for some time during the war to allow for the military training of ski paratroopers. Furthermore, the decision to build the model Habbakuk at the westernmost tip of Patricia

Lake, where there was no road access and barely a walking trail, assured officials that their classified experiment would remain confidential.

Today, the population of the town of Jasper and its surrounding municipality is more than 5200—it was considerably smaller back in 1943. Still, residents would have been curious about all the hush-hush activities taking place in their area. During the 50th anniversary celebrations of Project Habbakuk, in 1993, Nora Findlay told Mel Duvall of the *Calgary Herald* how frustrated she was that her husband Jim, an engineer with the town of Jasper in 1943, knew what was going on but was under strict instructions to keep that information confidential—even from his wife. Nora tried to do her own sleuthing and crept up to Patricia Lake on her own steam. But officials had planned for human curiosity, and the only access to the remote lake was well barricaded.

Once supplies were collected and delivered to Patricia Lake, the Canadian government had one more hoop to jump through—they needed the manpower to pull it off. But with the war waging, men in their prime with the strength and knowledge to get the job done weren't readily available. There were, however, a few exceptions.

Conscientious objectors were men with a pacifist view who refused, for religious reasons, to go to combat. During World War I, the Canadian government exempted these individuals from war service, but that changed during World War II when these men could serve overseas in a noncombatant capacity, working alongside medics for example, or building roads or working on farms in Canada. Most of these men chose to remain in Canada, not wanting to contribute to front line activities in any way, and served their country in what were called Alternative Service camps. As luck would have it, just such a camp was located right in Jasper.

With NRC scientists on hand to provide direction, and Jasper National Park superintendent Major J.A. Wood overseeing the project, 15 men from that Alternative Service camp worked around the clock for the better part of two months. They began by constructing a wooden box 18 metres long, 9 metres wide and 6 metres tall, complete with insulation and asphalt, on the frozen surface of Patricia Lake. Once the frame was built, metal piping, ductwork, Freon compressors and the layers of ice blocks cut and transported from Lake Louise were put in place.

By the end of March, the lake ice supporting the prototype was broke up to test if the scale model would float. To everyone's relief, it settled into the water to the appropriate depth and floated as planned. Work continued on the now floating test model, with layers of ice and insulating materials added, along with more ductwork and a refrigeration unit. Finally, in an effort to camouflage the bergship from anyone crafty enough to manage a closer look, a gable-type roof was installed to give the structure the appearance of a large houseboat. Some of the conscientious objectors involved in the project said that the boat looked like Noah's Ark, and a review of the detailed plans drawn up by the Montreal-based design team would seem to match this description.

The end product weighed 1000 tons. A one-horsepower engine ran the refrigeration unit and circulated the cool air.

Some say the prototype of the secret ice ship named Project Habbakuk, built in 1943, looked a little like Noah's Ark.

Aside from a single leak, which was eventually repaired, the bergship survived an entire summer floating on the lake unbeknownst to all but a few people.

A Leak in Security?

The best efforts don't always achieve perfect results. Was it possible that someone involved in the classified project at Patricia Lake leaked vital information, which, remarkably, made its way to the pages of DC Comics' popular serial *Superman*?

L.D. Cross, in her book *Code Name Habbakuk; A Secret Ship Made of Ice,* revealed a strange connection between what was happening on Patricia Lake and a couple of Canadian comic superstars Jerry Siegel and Joe Shuster. She explained that when A.E. Macdonald, head of civil engineering at the University of Manitoba, noticed a Superman comic with a tale that had whispers of the Habbakuk project, he forwarded it to the NRC in Ottawa. Although the comic book storyline seemed to hide what was really going on, it appeared to be an unbelievable coincidence that the comic strip referred to iceberg ships being constructed "somewhere in the Arctic [by] a group called the Hooded Men [who] used a laser gun to cut away icebergs." The storyline also included an atomic passenger liner carrying top-secret cargo on a collision course with a threatening iceberg, which was luring the liner with electromagnetic forces.

Were the comic geniuses mimicking real life, having somehow uncovered the top-secret project at Patricia Lake? The question plagued those involved with Habbakuk, but as it turned out, any concerns of a leak were unwarranted. The parallel between the comic strip and real life was indeed nothing more than coincidence; apparently the creative minds of Siegel and Shuster had pondered the power of ice as well.

Crunching the Numbers

Now that the prototype for a full-scale model was complete, operatives from Britain, the U.S., Canada and other Allied countries started to review what had been learned from the work completed in the spring of 1943. The pykrete was both light and buoyant and would withstand a great deal of abuse. Ice was free—a bonus since it contributed to a major portion of the ship's body. But a full-sized version of the Patricia Lake proto-type would need more than "280,000 super-ice pykrete blocks," which wasn't pure ice but a product requiring wood pulp and labour, "and require manpower approaching 8000 men" work-ing for "eight months." It was estimated that the production of these full-sized bergships would cost more than $100 million.

The data collected about what supplies would be needed and the costs of project as well as the tight timelines suggested by the Britain's Royal Navy, which wanted a bergship ready to go by the following year, left officials wondering whether it was all worth the effort. There were also concerns—during what would have been the construction phase of the bergship—that the weather wouldn't be cold enough to keep the ice in prime shape.

Mackenzie, who initially wrote in his journal about his concerns but dutifully managed Canada's commitment to the project, must have been overwhelmed with worry. From an out-sider's review of the story, there seemed to be no end to the stops and starts, no limit to the pros and cons, and no definitive direc-tion from anyone involved whether plans should proceed or cease.

To add to the mix, the tide had shifted in regard to the Battle of the Atlantic. Access to airstrips in Iceland and Portugal made it easier for Britain and the Allied powers to monitor threats in that area. There were other locations, however, where a berg-ship would be of great value, namely in the Pacific theatre and the war against Japan. Again, timelines and cost versus the value of the final project elicited so much controversy that no one wanted to make a final commitment to the project. Finally, in May 1943, Mackenzie made the tough decision and ended the Patricia Lake component of the Habbakuk project. Everything of value was stripped from the vessel, and the remaining shell was allowed to sink to the bottom of the once pristine mountain lake.

The future use of Habbakuk in other areas of the war was still somewhat up in the air, and the idea was revisited at several Combined Operations Headquarters (COHQ) conferences. At the Quebec Conference in August 1943, four months after the bergship prototype was dismantled, Mackenzie noted that Churchill was still very much in favour of backing the project. Despite the many setbacks, Churchill didn't throw in the towel on the bergship as soon as other Allied leaders had. Mountbatten attended the Quebec Conference in an attempt to get the Americans behind the idea of moving from a 1/50 scale model to creating a full-scale bergship.

To demonstrate its resilience, Mountbatten set up two frozen blocks, one made of pure ice and one of pykrete, drew his revolver, and pulled the trigger. The block of ice shattered. The bullet aimed at the pykrete simply ricocheted off and reverberated back to the surprised audience, nearly hitting an American admiral before falling to the ground.

As one writer put it in a 1997 article in the *Hamilton Spectator,* "That bizarre demonstration probably did as much to blow up Project Habbakuk as Mackenzie's staunch opposition to it." It wasn't until estimates placed the cost of a bergship at the six-million-pound mark that Churchill finally gave up the ghost.

In 1946, Mackenzie would publicly reflect on his experience at the helm of Habbakuk in a prepared speech: "[The bergships] occupied my personal attention most of my waking hours for four feverish months."

A Sunken Secret

Although the story of Project Habbakuk was no longer a secret after warring factions ceased their fire and an armistice was signed, the general public knew nothing of the saga. An article from the UK's Royal Naval Museum Library suggests that it wasn't until the 1970s that divers delved into the chilly waters of Patricia Lake and located the remains of the project in its watery graveyard. The cold water has preserved much of the materials used to build the ship. Divers who have visited the site attest that little has changed from year to year, providing that visitors leave the area untouched.

Project Habbakuk is truly a one-of-a-kind shipwreck, making it a priceless remnant of a war that should never be forgotten. Diving enthusiasts and history buffs are encouraged to visit the site where Canada's contribution to supporting the Allied forces, and the vision of one genius, was first realized. But as representatives from the Alberta Underwater Alliance, Alberta Underwater Archaeology Society, and Parks Canada would all caution, take no souvenirs and leave nothing behind. Keeping the area intact helps to ensure that this mysterious World War II story stays alive for future visitors to discover.

Chapter Sixteen

Turning the Pages of History:
The Bar U Ranch

~

Two Percherons snort at each other as a crew loads a grey and weathered wagon. A dozen people, plus the driver, fit on this flatbed, and the black beauties harnessed to this clapboard vehicle snort a few more times before they begin their pull from the tourist centre to the place that visitors have come to see—the Bar U Ranch.

Making their way along the winding road that leads to what looks like a little village nestled in front of the much larger backdrop of the Rocky Mountains, visitors can immerse themselves in a way of life that, today, is largely forgotten. There are no frills here—no modern conveniences or louvered windows or metal roofs. The Bar U Ranch looks the same as it did during its heyday, providing visitors with a taste of the Old West they can't experience anywhere else.

"The oldest building on site is the saddle horse barn, which was constructed in about 1885," the driver says, pointing to one structure. According to Bruce Stephenson,

interpretive guide and visitor concierge, most of the buildings were built some time between 1882, when the ranch was first established, and early 1937. Stephenson goes on to explain that the last building constructed was the tractor shed, which was built in 1937.

Of Canada's 65 class one historic buildings, 32 are located at the Bar U Ranch. With their structural integrity intact, 26 of those buildings are still being used—the homes, barns, sheds and offices were built to last. "Aside from these buildings, nothing has been built on the historic site or brought in for show," Stephenson said. "And if we lose a building to fire or some other [disaster], it will not be replaced."

To one side of the property a young cowboy pokes at an open fire. "Would you like some coffee? Tea?" he asks those passing by. At another building, located south and east of the cowboy's campsite is the ranch's cookhouse. In the backyard the "cook," dressed in a period costume, is picking and cleaning vegetables from the ranch's large garden. "Have a carrot," she offers. It's crisp, sweet and puts the skinned baby carrots in grocery stores to shame.

After a quick tutorial on the ins and outs of what life was like at Bar U during its prime when it occupied 52 square kilometres of ranchland, it's no mystery why the ranch was so successful. This rural business ran like a well-oiled machine.

But that doesn't mean the Bar U Ranch doesn't harbour a few surprises. Along with the weathered buildings, the rusted iron door handles, antique metal wheels and rickety hand-pump wells, there are the whispers of lives long since ended who have left their mark on this patch of land. And one of the people who visited the Bar U was none other than Butch Cassidy's sidekick, the Sundance Kid.

~

During its 130-year history, the Bar U Ranch made a name for itself as one of the most successful cattle ranches in the West. In fact, it was considered one of the most successful ranching operations in all of Canada for more than 70 years, running 30,000 head of cattle and 1000 Percheron horses during its most productive era. The ranch's solid start was largely the result of one young man's vision and the Canadian government's offer of a 21-year lease "on a maximum of 100,000 acres of land for a penny an acre."

Canada was still a young and largely unexplored country when 36-year-old Fred Stimson felt the call to go west. By then, he'd already proven his business prowess, having taken over his family's Compton County farm in southeastern Quebec after his father, Arba, died. With his older brother, Charles, gainfully employed as a "merchant and manufacturer of leather goods" in nearby Montreal, the role fell naturally to Fred who, at 18, was the next oldest offspring.

The Stimson family had connections to affluent families in the east, and Fred made good use of those connections. Less than a decade after taking on his burgeoning responsibilities, Fred took out a $6000 loan from Sir Hugh Allan, a Canadian financier and shipping magnate with a true Scottish penchant for money management. The loan was used to update their farm buildings, which by that point were in sore need of modernization. Stimson repaid his debt in short order, further demonstrating his own excellent business prowess. So when Fred, once again, approached Sir Hugh with a business proposition to purchase a considerable parcel of land and a large herd of cattle in what would become Alberta a few years later, Allan gave him an ear.

In the end, Allan was one of several businessmen who financially backed Stimson's venture in the west, but Stimson had the vision, the energy and the drive to establish the North West Cattle Company, and he set the foundation for making Bar U Ranch into the success it became.

Stimson travelled to the vast prairie land skirting the Rocky Mountains, and because of his business acumen, chose the location for the Bar U Ranch. By the time the final paperwork was signed, investors had come and gone, but in March 1882, the North West Cattle Company was firmly established and reigned for the next 20 years.

The Mystery Behind the Man

Although Fred Stimson was the ranch's chief executive officer, he wasn't really the typical cowboy-type of fellow that you might think would establish a ranch. In *The Bar U and Canadian Ranching History*, author Simon M. Evans writes that a photograph of Stimson on a horse is virtually non-existent. Stimson wasn't an avid outdoorsman in any sense of the definition. And he wasn't much into roughing it, either.

Most of the original buildings and much of the farming implements used at the Bar U Ranch have been preserved in their original state.

Initially, Stimson envisioned being a financial partner in this ranching business, but by the time the ranch was up and running, he was relegated to the position of manager. He was little more than a valued employee with a 10-percent share in the company and a strong vision—not at all what he expected, considering the biggest lure in the entire venture must have been a blend of adventure mixed with the possibility of an ever-growing financial reward.

History is silent about the persona of Fred Stimson, making him somewhat of an enigma, but one can guess what motivated him to create one of the most successful ranching operations in Canadian history—some of his choices during and following his 21-year tenure at the Bar U Ranch suggest he wasn't afraid to speculate into the unknown. For example, it is somewhat surprising that he seemed to prefer the comforts of prosperity to a life on the range.

Stimson closely aligned himself with the Stoney and Blackfoot peoples living in the area, and he actively participated in their culture. He acquired their clothes, including a headdress of his very own, and learned to speak the Blackfoot language. He hired these men as range riders, and he was a voice for Native rights at a time when Canada's First Nations peoples were most misunderstood. In addition, there were hints that Stimson may have had a Native wife, and Native offspring—apparently it wasn't unheard of for white settlers at that point in Alberta's history to have two wives, one from their culture and a Native wife.

When the 21-year lease was up, the ranch was sold to George Lane, an ambitious young ranch hand who'd worked with the company since 1884. Lane and an assortment of business partners are credited with taking the ranch through perhaps its most prosperous era. That meant Stimson was without a job, but he didn't let that dampen his spirits too much. He just pulled up his socks and moved south to Cuba, where he managed a ranch for William Van Horne for a time.

Meanwhile, Lane took over the responsibilities of running the ranch. Unlike Stimson, Lane was a hands-on person.

According to the Parks Canada visitor's guide, Lane "came to Alberta to work for this very outfit. He struck the country with exactly $100 and started to work for the Bar U outfit for $100 a month...[and] he has by his own unaided efforts become one of the most wealthy and substantial men in Alberta."

Somewhere between the time Stimson was on his way out and Lane was establishing himself as the lead man at the ranch, a particularly colourful character made his way over from the U.S. with the thoughts of starting a new life with a new, wholesome focus, and in doing so, landed himself a job as a ranch hand at the Bar U Ranch.

That young man called himself the Sundance Kid.

One of the Wild Bunch

Harry Alonzon Longabaugh was born in Pennsylvania sometime between 1867 and 1870—sources differ as to his year of birth. He was the youngest of five children, and it seems that he had a typical home life. But Harry took Horace Greeley's advice to "Go West, young man, go West" quite literally, and shortly after his 14th birthday, Harry hit the road and started making his way across the United States.

Although he may have been given all the tools any youngster needs to live the good life, young Harry had a penchant for the wild side. By the time he was 20, he'd already been in trouble with the law for stealing a gun, horse and saddle from the town of Sundance, Wyoming. He spent 18 months behind bars for his shenanigans, but his incarceration clearly didn't deter him much since he adopted the town's name as his moniker, and just for good measure added "Kid" for the punch line. Perhaps this was his tribute to Billy the Kid, the infamous outlaw of the time who died in a hail of bullets in 1881. Or maybe Harry Longabaugh knew he couldn't drive the straight path for long. But when he was released, he tried to give it the old college try.

In her book, *The Sundance Kid: The Life of Harry Alonzo Longabaugh*, Donna Ernst explains how Longabaugh (a distant relative of hers) headed into Canada in the fall of 1889, following his stint in jail, and landed at the Bar U Ranch. As luck would have it—or maybe Longabaugh planned it this way all along—the Sundance Kid connected with Cyril Everett "Ebb" Johnson. Johnson and Longabaugh were friends from before the time of Longabaugh's troubles with the law, and Johnson knew the kid had the kind of ranching skills he was looking for. At that point in Bar U's history, the ranch boasted a herd of more than 10,000 cattle and more than 800 horses. Sundance's expertise was in breaking horses.

Not a lot is written about Longabaugh's time at the Bar U. Most of the literature about this mysterious character focuses on his unlawful exploits south of the border. But Ernst does point out that ranch staff both liked and respected the young man. In addition, Ernst pulls insights into the cowboy's character from the memoirs of a man named Fred Ings, who was employed at the nearby 76 Ranch around the same time Sundance was at the Bar U.

According to his memoirs, Ings acknowledged Longabaugh's skill as a "splendid rider and a top notch cow hand," but he also admits he suspected Sundance was evading the law in the US. Still, while Sundance was around, Ings suggests the ranch hand was a "decent fine fellow who could not have been better behaved." Longabaugh once demonstrated his compassion by backtracking in a blizzard to find Ings who was riding herd with him at the time, ensuring the man made it safely back to camp.

Unfortunately, try as he might, Sundance couldn't shake his bad-boy reputation altogether. A few people didn't like the man—they sensed a no-good core in that shiny apple he presented to the public. And in August 1891, he was arrested after someone reported him for mistreating a horse. Those charges were dropped, and Sundance kept his job—for the time being, anyway. By 1892, Sundance was trying his own hand at business, partnering with a man named Frank Hamilton at the Grand Central Hotel Saloon in nearby Calgary. But that partnership was short-lived, and it wasn't long before Sundance was on his way back to the States.

It seems that life started taking a downward turn for Longabaugh at this point.

By 1892, Sundance was a suspect in a train robbery, followed by a bank holdup five years later. He was photographed with a group of young hooligans, one of whom was the infamous Robert Parker, aka Butch Cassidy, and the group of five who started hanging out together and named themselves the "Wild Bunch." Life was extremely tumultuous. Ings, along with the other ranch hands who knew and liked Sundance, read news stories of their friend's exploits and were concerned. "We all felt sorry when he left and got in bad again across the line."

It wasn't hard to feel sorry for Sundance who, although he struggled with adhering to the precepts of the law, seemed nice enough—loveable even.

Historians disagree about what actually happened to Harry Longabaugh. Many suggest he was killed in a gunfight in Bolivia in 1908 after he and Butch Cassidy scammed a local mining company's payroll. Two bodies were recovered following that gunfight—whether the men died as a result of the lawmen cornering them or by their own hand is unclear. In any case, the bodies were never identified before they were buried. And Pinkerton's, a detective agency based in Chicago in 1850, never completely believed the Sundance Kid and Butch Cassidy died that day.

Pinkerton's wasn't alone. Several sources questioned whether the bodies buried after that shootout were indeed Sundance and Cassidy. For one thing, the two outlaws might have been bad guys in the strictest sense of the word, but they weren't killers—the first time they could have been accused of physical force was during that shootout in Bolivia. For another thing, the bodies uncovered after that faceoff were never officially identified. Furthermore, sightings of Butch Cassidy and the Sundance Kid were reported on several occasions thereafter; Butch apparently attended several family gatherings, and over the years, suspicion mounted that Longabaugh assumed a new identity and lived his days out in Duchesne, Utah, under the alias William Henry Long.

Investigators bent on confirming the fate of these two outlaws have also searched out their graves at the San Vicente cemetery where the outlaws in the shootout were supposed to be buried. No one has been able to unearth the remains of anyone with DNA matching either men.

And so it is that the fate of the Sundance Kid remains unknown. Is it possible he and Butch Cassidy survived the gunfight in Bolivia? And if they did, who were the victims pulled from the carnage and buried in their place? Is it possible that the pair, who weren't known for their violence, was never part of the shootout in the first place? Perhaps they were nothing more than petty criminals looking for a sure bet to provide for their golden years? Maybe—just maybe—the men recognized they could no longer run together and finally parted ways. Parker allegedly maintained his connections to his family, albeit in a flimsy manner, while Longabaugh kept a larger distance between himself and his kin.

Did Longabaugh and the love of his life, Etta Place, live out their golden years in a secluded and remote cabin somewhere? Is it possible that the couple might have moved back to Alberta, where Harry could have maintained a low profile without too much difficulty? After all, the amiable Sundance had a good many friends who still stood by him and believed that he was, in the end, a "decent fine fellow who could not have been better behaved."

Some questions in history remain a mystery. What exactly happened to the Sundance Kid and the extent of his connection to this province is one of those questions.

On Another Note

The Bar U Ranch didn't just attract some of history's more questionable characters. The Wild West of Canada called out to adventurers from all walks of life, including, as it so happens, royalty.

In 1919, Edward VIII, Prince of Wales, purchased the Bedingfield Ranch. George Lane arranged the purchase of the property, located not far from the Bar U Ranch. The Prince of Wales renamed the property the "E.P. Ranch" and planned to use it for both personal pleasure and business matters. Despite the prince's professed intentions for the property, Paul Leonard Voisley, author of *High River and the Times: An Alberta Community and its Weekly Newspaper*, points out that the prince issued "a souvenir booklet, catered to touring groups, and even allowed curious individuals to roam about providing they caused no damage, closed all gates, and left no garbage."

When a prince purchases a property and makes that purchase public, neighbouring residents expect to see him from time to time. Unfortunately, Edward VIII did not satisfy in this regard. For 43 years Edward owned the 41-hectare ranch, located near Pekisko Creek. But aside from limited visits in the 1920s and the occasional visit with his wife Wallis Simpson in the 1940s and 1950s following his abdication from the throne,

Edward was notably absent. In 1962 the Duke of Windsor sold his Canadian interest to "Jim Cartwright, of High River's D Ranch." The E.P. Ranch is now listed as one of Canada's official Historic Places.

Perhaps it was the longevity of the Bar U Ranch that inevitably opened it up to contact with so many different people over the years. Then again, it may have been that the appearances of characters like Sundance, or Prince Edward, for that matter, had nothing to do with the ranch at all—they just appeared, coincidentally.

Either way, it's obvious that there's just something about Alberta that attracts all kinds of people, some of whom have added to the colourful tapestry of our province.

Conclusion

When I first embarked on the journey to unearth some of Alberta's most baffling mysteries, I didn't have to struggle to come up with a list of story ideas. However, it quickly became evident that there were just too many ideas, and I couldn't possibly do all of the stories justice within the confines of this book. What to include, and what to put away for a second volume down the road became the conundrum I had to resolve, and I knew that no matter what I chose, I wouldn't be completely satisfied with the result.

That's where this part of the book comes into the picture—it's my chance to mention a few of the other mysteries I would have loved to research and write about.

Did you know...

There is a 199-hectare piece of land 48 kilometres north of Fort McMurray near the hamlet of Fort MacKay that is a burial site of extensive archaeological significance. Spear points dating back 9000 years have been discovered in the area, but until recently the quarry containing the type of stone required to make these particular artifacts had never been found. Now, the "Quarry of the Ancestors" is beginning to reveal the mysteries of a time in Canadian history that not much is known about.

Head-Smashed-in Buffalo Jump is a world heritage site with "one of the world's oldest, largest and best preserved buffalo jumps." Although much is known about the plains people who once lived here, mysteries remain to be unearthed.

According to the website of Writing-on-Stone Provincial Park, the park near Lethbridge contains the "largest concentration of First Nation petroglyphs (rock carvings) and pictographs

For nearly 6000 years, Native peoples of the North American Plains migrated to what is now known as Head-Smashed-in Buffalo Jump for their annual buffalo hunt. The UNESCO World Heritage Site represented a gold mine for archaeologists to "unraveling the mysteries of ancient aboriginals." Above the cliffs where the buffalo met their fate is a holy site not open to the public.

(rock paintings) on the great plains of North America." What motivated Canada's First Nations people to choose this place as their unique art gallery?

Rumours of mountains full of silver ready for the taking drew an estimated 3000 people, mostly miners, to Castle Mountain. Three communities sprang up in the area: Siding 29 (now Banff) and Holt City (now Lake Louise) weathered the storms, even though the promise of silver turned out to be nothing more than a scam, and the third community, Silver City, disappeared. Granted, the strange little town didn't have many stores, churches or schools. It did boast six casino-hotels, all of which were dismantled and reassembled in other nearby towns and villages. What was the story behind the silver scam, and why, of the three upstart communities, does only a plaque remain to commemorate what many once hoped would be a prosperous city?

And then there's the story about a nosey golden retriever named Arthur who unearthed a "mystery animal mummy" near his owner's home in Craigmyle. The word is still out on a positive identification of the strange creature.

When it comes to mysterious, quirky people, Harry Cooper is definitely someone to check out. It's not clear exactly how tall this giant of a man was, but he was hailed as the "world's tallest man" when he worked the circus circuit in 1899. Unfortunately, the kindly gent died while touring Alberta and was buried in Calgary. One-hundred-and-five years would pass before his grave got a marker—his actual height, however, remains a mystery.

On the sadder side of life, there is the mysterious disappearance of 20-year-old Amber Tuccaro. The woman went missing on August 18, 2010, after catching a ride to Edmonton from Nisku, where she was staying in a hotel with her son and a friend. The authorities haven't given up on explaining the mysterious disappearance of this young woman, whose remains were found in September 2012, or finding the man they believe may have abducted her. Just as this book was going to press, police released a video, complete with a voice recording of a conversation between Amber and the man who was supposed to be driving her to the city, in the hope that someone who hears the recording might be able to identify the male voice. Surely Amber's child deserves justice in this case.

As I mentioned in the introduction to this book, stories that raise questions in our minds or leave us wanting to learn more can qualify as a mystery or, at the very least, contain mysterious elements. Based on that definition, there is no shortage of mystery in Alberta.

Notes on Sources

General Sources

Information for stories throughout this book was retrieved from numerous sources, including several community news outlets, online and print publications, and special interest groups:

Aboriginal Multi-Media Society (AMMS)

Alberta Parks

Alberta Provincial Police Archives

Alberta Rural Development Network

American Merchant Marine at War (www.usmm.org)

Atlas Coal Mine Society

BBC (British Broadcasting Corporation)

BLT Research

Calgary Herald

Canada's Historic Places, A Federal, Provincial and Territorial Collaboration

Canadianbadlands.com

The Canadian Encyclopedia online

The Canadian UFO Survey

CBC (Canadian Broadcasting Corporation)

Bill Casselman

City of Medicine Hat

Edmonton Journal

Frank Slide Interpretive Centre

Glenbow Archives

Globe and Mail

Google Earth

Head-Smashed-in Buffalo Jump World Heritage Site

International Council of Professional Therapists

Lac Ste. Anne Mission

Lacombe Globe

Library and Archives Canada

Montreal Gazette

Murderpedia

The National Post

Oblate Communications, The Missionary Oblates of Mary Immaculate
Our Future, Our Past, The Alberta Heritage Digitization Project
Parks Canada,
Postmedia News
Project KARE
Quebecor Media Inc.
The Report (also known as *Alberta Report*)
The RiverWatch Institute of Alberta
Royal Canadian Mounted Police
Royal Naval Museum
Royal Tyrrell Museum
St. Albert Gazette
Statistics Canada
Sun Media
Sydney Morning Herald
Toronto Star
Travel Drumheller
Ufology Research
Vancouver Sun
The Weather Network
The Western Catholic Reporter
Wikipedia
Bruce Wishart

Specific Sources

Anderson, Frank. *The Frank Slide Story*. Aldergrove, BC: Frontier Publishing, 1979.

Anderson, Frank. *Tragedies of the Crowsnest Pass*. Surrey, BC: Frontier Books, 1983.

"The Badlands: Living History, Where the Past is a Path to the Future." Discovery Alberta: A *Calgary Herald* Magazine Series Exploring Our Geography and Special Places. Issue 4, 2005/2006.

Burns, R.W. *The Life and Times of A.D. Blumlein*. London: Institution of Electrical Engineers (IEE) in association with the Science Museum, 2000.

Cross, L.D. *Amazing Stories, Code Name Habbakuk: A Secret Ship Made of Ice*. Victoria, Vancouver, Calgary: Heritage House, 2012.

Ernst, D.B. *The Sundance Kid: The Life of Harry Alonzo Longabaugh*. Norman, OK: University of Oklahoma Press, 2012.

Evans, S.M. *The Bar U and Canadian Ranching History.* Calgary, AB: University of Calgary Press, 2004.

Horan, J.W. *On the Side of the Law: Biography of J.D. Nicholson.* Edmonton, AB: The Institute of Applied Art, 1944.

Johnston, Basil. *The Manitous: The Spiritual World of the Ojibway.* Toronto, ON: Key Porter Books, 1995.

Kerr, J. William. *Frank Slide.* Calgary, AB: Barker Publishing, 1990.

Leonard, David. "Murder on the Prairie: Who Killed the Six Immigrant Settlers?" *Alberta History,* Vol. 58, No. 4, 2010.

Plett, Jake. *Valley of Shadows.* Beaverlodge, AB: Horizon House Publishers, 1975.

Riley, Dan, Tom Primrose and Hugh Dempsey. *Frontier Series No. 4. The Lost Lemon Mine: The Great Mystery of the Canadian Rockies.* Victoria, Vancouver, Calgary: Heritage House, 1980.

Smith, Barbara. *Deadly Encounters: True Crime Stories of Alberta.* Toronto, ON: Hounslow Press (Dundurn Press), 1993.

Smith, Barbara. *Ghost Stories of Alberta.* Toronto, ON: Dundurn Press, 1993.

Smith, Barbara. *Haunted Alberta: 62 True Ghost Stories.* Edmonton, AB: Lone Pine Publishing, 2009.

Stewart, Ron. *Amazing Stories, The Lost Lemon Mine, An Unsolved Mystery of the Old West.* Victoria, Vancouver, Calgary: Heritage House, 2011.

Lisa Wojna

Bestselling author Lisa Wojna has at least 26 nonfiction books to her credit, including five previous works published with Quagmire Press: *Missing! The Disappeared, Lost or Abducted in Canada, Unsolved Murders of Canada, Canadian Con Artists, Canada's Most Wanted* and *Identity Theft in Canada*. She has worked in the community newspaper industry as a writer and journalist and has travelled all over Canada and even to the wilds of Africa. Although writing and photography have been a central part of her life for as long as she can remember, it's the people behind every story that are her motivation and give her the most fulfilment.